THE BOOM
IN SPANISH AMERICAN LITERATURE
A Personal History

 Center
for
Inter-American
Relations

A Center for Inter-American Relations Book

THE BOOM
IN
SPANISH AMERICAN
LITERATURE
A Personal History

BY JOSÉ DONOSO

Translated by Gregory Kolovakos

Published by
COLUMBIA UNIVERSITY PRESS
in association with the
CENTER FOR INTER-AMERICAN RELATIONS
New York 1977

Library of Congress Cataloging in Publication Data

Donoso, José, 1924–
The boom in Spanish American literature.

Translation of Historia personal del "boom."
1. Spanish American fiction—20th century—History
and criticism.   I. Center for Inter-American Relations.
II. Title.
PQ7081.D6313   863   76-53747
ISBN 0-231-04164-0
ISBN 0-231-04165-9 pbk.

For Yves and Bignia Zimmermann

FOREWORD

As I WRITE, I have lying on my desk a letter from Victoria Ocampo, who sends me clippings from a recent Argentine newspaper proclaiming the death of the Boom in Latin American fiction and denouncing the methods that Boom authors have used to gain their fame. This letter (from the woman who founded the publishing house and the literary review named SUR in order to promote the recognition and internationalization of Latin American culture) and these clippings (by a journalist eager to defame the most celebrated cluster of writers in Latin American literary history) are fitting signs for the beginning and end—or ends—of the history that José Donoso tells in this small volume. Signs indicating the growing fame that quickly became a notoriety and an existence chiefly known, like that of vampires, for its incessant deaths.

Like the novel itself, a genre that constitutes its principal product, the Boom resists definition and explanation. Consequently, many say that there never was such a thing. But as we have come to recognize the very nature of the novel in its perpetual resurrections, so may we glimpse the nature of the Boom: if it has died—once again—this amorphous creature had to be alive, at least in some form, in order to accomplish that terminal act. Postulating its existence from a morbid hindsight, then, I may be able, without abducting facts and perceptions from Donoso's narrative, to say something that will orient the North American reader toward Donoso's subject.

During the 1960s in Latin America there appeared in different countries, and almost simultaneously, a number of novels and collections of short stories that by their virtuoso technique and style dazzled a large reading public that almost no one had even guessed was there. This sudden flowering of writers like Carlos Fuentes, Julio Cortázar, and Mario Vargas Llosa won even more attention because these same writers began, almost at once, to be translated into foreign languages and to put Latin America on the international literary map for the first time. Spoken and written about with admiration and envy, the phenomenon quickly came to be known as the Boom, a corollary metaphor to the equally ugly but customary "literary stock market." The label conferred a unity where there may have been none and a connotation more powerfully economic than esthetic. (Think of the chance collection of poets we call Romantics as the Rush or of that other nongroup we call the Decadents as the Crash and you will have some sense of the ambiguities and distortions implicit in the label "Boom.")

Because North American publishers are often reluctant to take on works of translation, because the reading public for such works in this country is relatively small—one reason may be the cause of the other, but in which order no one can tell—the Boom did not reach us until the late '60s and the early '70s. To give some sense of how far behind the times we have been—a sense of what some will want to call *our* "culture lag"—you need only remember that John Barth's historic essay "The Literature of Exhaustion" appeared in the *Atlantic Monthly* in 1967. This essay is a unique document in the history of U.S.–Latin American literary relations since it marks the first time that one of our major novelists openly admits a Latin American writer, Jorge Luis Borges, to an influence on North American literature. (Previously the circumstance was always— and not always inaccurately—reversed, with many books studying the influence of Poe or, more notably, of Whitman on Latin American writers.) If we take Barth's major statement as a turning point, we must also remember that 1967 marks a point almost a full twenty years after Borges had written his most important fiction and a point two-thirds of the way through the decade of the Boom. Like most things dazzlingly up-to-date, Barth's essay was already out-of-date—from a crudely historical point of view—by the time he published it. In the years since 1967 our writers, our critics, our students and teachers have responded to these translations from Latin America with increasing wonder and pleasure. Books like Gabriel García Márquez' *One Hundred Years of Solitude* and Julio Cortázar's *Hopscotch* have become near-classics for both readers and writers, and the conjunction of Robert Coover and José Donoso on the front page of *The New York Times Book*

Review in the North American's praising review of the Chilean novelist's masterwork, *The Obscene Bird of Night*, is both an omen and a confirmation.

A figure within the Boom of the Latin American novel himself, Donoso is able to write this short "history" from the close-up, first-person point of view. Of course he gives dates, lists places and people, but what really counts here is his first-hand experience and insight written in a chatty, casual style different from anything in his remarkable novels. Pointedly beginning the Boom's career with a party—and ending it with one as well—Donoso shuns the scholar's formal parade of literary history—keeps clear of the invidious quality that drives such scholars to calling everyone else's description stupid—and more than compensates with his novelist's attention to detail, his story-teller's gift for exposition by anecdote, his writer's ultimate concern with the psychology of the action he narrates, especially with the express development of his most interesting character's mind—in this case, Donoso's. Not the definitive historian of the Boom, not even trying to be, Donoso has written a unique document about the Boom which, at the same time, figures in the literature of that Boom.

For us, Donoso's small book provides the chance to catch up on our literary history without being lectured to; it also offers an opportunity to understand the internationalization of a literature in which we are increasingly participating, and that internationalization, as Donoso makes clear, is as much what the Boom signifies as anything else. For the first time, Latin American writers are taking part in the universal dialogue of literature and for the first time we are really listening to them. If the Boom itself is over, it has succeeded in doing what Victoria Ocampo's literary review SUR began in the 1930s: introducing the foreign—whether home-grown or imported—both at home and abroad as a means to having the world culture that is the birthright of all of us.

Letter and clipping, then—family tree and death certificate—are fitting signs of what may be either a phase or a singular phenomenon, a process or a completed event. No matter. Whatever else, the Boom is such a clustering of genius as seldom witnessed by anyone, even less frequently testified to by one of the participants.

RONALD CHRIST

May 1976
New York

THE BOOM
IN SPANISH AMERICAN LITERATURE
A Personal History

. . . the final beauty of writing is never felt by contemporaries; but they ought, I think, to be bowled over . . .

Virginia Woolf, *A Writer's Diary*

Give me envy as large as a mountain, and I shall give you a reputation as large as the world . . .

Benito Pérez Galdós, *The Disinherited*

I

I WANT TO BEGIN these notes by venturing the opinion that if the Spanish American novel of the 1960s has come to have that debatably unified existence known as the Boom, it is due, more than anything else, to those who have devoted themselves to disputing it; and that, real or fictitious, valuable or negligible, but always entangled with the unlikely carnival that has overtaken it, the Boom is a creation of hysteria, envy, and paranoia. If it were not, the public would be content to consider Spanish American prose fiction—excluding some works and including others, according to personal taste—as having achieved an extraordinary high point in the past decade.

During the '60s in Latin America, many novels were

written of a quality that, from the moment of their appearance right up to the present, I have thought undeniable; novels that, for historical and cultural circumstances, have merited international attention—from Mexico to Argentina, from Cuba to Uruguay. These works have had and continue to have a literary repercussion never before witnessed in the modern novel as written in Spanish. If Blasco Ibáñez, for example, had a cosmopolitan repercussion in his time, no one has ever pretended that his was anything more than commercial literature.[1] And I want to emphasize that I am speaking of what is specifically literary, not of the number of copies sold, which is only one element of that repercussion: it is sufficient to compare the astonishing sales of *One Hundred Years of Solitude* to the very limited sales of *Paradiso*—both, undoubtedly, members of the very first rank in the hypothetical Boom. In comparison to their German, North American, French, and English contemporaries, the great names of the "literary" novel written in Spanish during the first half of this century—just as many Latin Americans as Spaniards—have disappeared without leaving any great impression on the formation of the present novelists.

What, then, is the Boom? What is there of truth and of fraud in it? Undoubtedly it is difficult to define with even moderate rigor this literary phenomenon which has recently ended—if it really has ended—and whose existence as a unity is due not to the arbitrariness of those writers

---

[1] Vicente Blasco Ibáñez (1867–1928) was a Spanish novelist who began with novels of naturalism based in Valencia (*The Cabin*, 1898, and *Reeds and Mud*, 1902). He later turned to novels which gave him great popularity and financial success, novels such as *Blood and Sand*, 1909, and *The Four Horsemen of the Apocalypse*, 1916, based on World War I. [G.K.]

who may be a part of it, not to its undying loyalties of friendship; but, rather, to the invention of those who question it. In any case, maybe it is worthwhile to begin by pointing out that on the simplest level and prior to possible, and possibly accurate, historical and cultural explanations, there exists the fortuitous circumstance that on the same continent, in twenty-one republics where more or less recognizable varieties of Spanish are written, and during a period of a very few years, there appeared both the brilliant first novels by authors who matured very or relatively early—Vargas Llosa and Carlos Fuentes, for example—and the major novels by older, prestigious authors—Ernesto Sábato, Onetti, Cortázar—which thus produced a spectacular conjunction. In a period of scarcely six years, between 1962 and 1968, I read *The Death of Artemio Cruz*, *The Time of the Hero*, *The Green House*, *The Shipyard*, *Paradiso*, *Hopscotch*, *Sobre héroes y tumbas* (About Heroes and Tombs), *One Hundred Years of Solitude*, and other novels all recently published at that time.[2] Suddenly, there burst into view about a dozen novels, noteworthy at the very least and populating a previously uninhabited space.

That is the neutral fact, exactly as the card catalogs of literary history record it. But in English the word "boom" has nothing neutral about it. On the contrary, it is charged with connotations, nearly all of them pejorative or suspicious, except, perhaps, in recognizing expansiveness and superabundance. "Boom" is an onomatopoeia that signifies explosion; but time has added to it a sense of falsity, of an eruption coming from nothing, containing little and leav-

---

[2] English titles are used for translated works and English equivalents are given in parentheses for untranslated works. [G.K.]

3

ing less. It implies, above all, that this brief and hollow duration is necessarily accompanied by deceit and corruption, by a lack of quality and by exploitation—as in *Mahagonny* by Bertolt Brecht. Quite probably, the first people to apply this epithet to the recent Latin American novel did not want to signify anything praiseworthy. And those who avidly popularized the term were even less concerned with merit.

As for the rest, no one, neither the critics, the public, the salesmen, nor the writers, has ever agreed on what novelists and which novels belong to the Boom. What are the political and esthetic passwords? Which are the accepted prizes, publishing houses, literary agents, critics, and reviews, and for how long and under what conditions has this acceptance lasted? Which are the insignia and emblems? Who distributes them and in what parts of the world—Buenos Aires, Havana, New York, Paris, Barcelona, Mexico City—is this distribution carried out? And in the event that anyone accepts the present or past existence of the Boom, no one is ready to adopt it, defining the manner in which he became conscious of that existence. On the other hand, no one knows whether it can be asserted that the fortunate explosion is over. The Boom of the contemporary Spanish American novel enjoys a strange polemical existence which does not solidify into any true polemic because no one wants to decide which side of the fence he is on—or even if there is a fence. All that remains is a steady stream of rumors and quarrels started by the most varied kinds of detractors. The truth is that these detractors, frightened by the possibility of finding themselves excluded or of having to prove that their countries did not have names worthy of the honor roll, threw a sheet over the specter of their fear and, having covered it up, defined its fluctuating and frightening form. So the Boom was invented: in this way the detractors took it from the world of literature and introduced it into the world of publicity and hubbub. And in this way they have kept the Boom's supposed unity in the public eye, lavishing upon those authors the same free publicity which they accuse the members of the Boom of being so skillful in getting for themselves, since, like Mafia bosses, the authors are supposed to manage the pool of secrets which assure success. As with a mirage, these detractors are the only ones who believe in the monolithic unity of the Boom: that impenetrable, proud Freemasonry, that society of mutual praise, that privileged caste which capriciously and cruelly passes judgment on the names of those who should and should not belong . . . nobody quite knows why. . . .

Slanderers of the Boom come in every shape and color. Perhaps the ones who jabber most are those who believe themselves to be unjustly pushed to the sidelines by the dictators who refuse to let them in. In reprisal, they devote themselves to what has come to be called "the literary *trottoir*"; that is, to gaining prestige by means of hostile articles and lectures. There are also the pedants who, bent over texts and brandishing names in their flaccid, sweaty hands, prove the absence of any "total literary originality," an originality which no serious novelist would want to claim for his work. There are the dangerous personal enemies who extend their hatred to the whole group which their paranoid imaginations have created. There are the fools who, having published a first book honored by an insignificant prize, assure the press that they are now part of the Boom and make statements in the name of a group

5

which does not exist while, if it did, its members would have the most disparate positions. There are the envious and the failures: a professor who wanted to be a novelist and failed, a decayed bureaucrat in his little international job. There are the naïve people who believe everything, who support everything, who praised the Boom when it was first spoken of but did not think to predict its scope, then denied its value and even its existence, and now firmly believe in the death of something whose existence they had denied. There are those bedazzled by a supposed *glamour* in the style of fashion designers: "the unresisted temptation, the vanity of the jet set, the agreeable double-chin from an author's fat royalties, the splendid intoxication from martinis toasting the health of the Fellinis. . . ." And there is also the unique phenomenon of a man of the stature of Miguel Angel Asturias, who felt the moss of time beginning to shroud his rhetoric of blood-sweat-and-tears, and attempted to defend himself during a lecture in Salamanca by alluding to plagiarism and stating that the current novelists are "mere products of publicity."

Perhaps some of the most curious phenomena are certain of the national attitudes toward the hypothetical Boom: Argentina is so rich in second-rate writers—in addition to her many writers of the first rank—that a separate Olympus has been established there, a highly esteemed national Boom or "*petit* Boom" (as they would be likely to say) with its own roster and its own particular judgments and values: many are dismissed for not being an author "sufficiently known among us." Chile, on the other hand, during the '60s contented itself with being a country that "has no novelists"—it is, undoubtedly, a land of poets—and before justified political passion relegated literary passions to a secondary position, there was a shameful attitude in just this sense: a terrible blue-stocking, with a very snobbish background in Chile, took the trouble to come, without an invitation, to my home in Vallvidrera, Barcelona, one winter afternoon while I was frenetically attempting to finish *The Obscene Bird of Night*, in order to repeat to me that cliché which had the grace to paralyze me as a writer for a month: "Chile has no novelists." And in Spain a curious attitude, both painful and ambivalent, has existed toward the Boom: admiration and scorn, competition and hospitality. The Spanish attitude is rather complex and serious, something which would be very instructive if it were analyzed. In any case, for no other country does the Boom have such a distinct existence as it does for Spain.

I should make it clear that it is not the intention of these notes to define the Boom. I do not want to set myself up as its historian, chronicler, or critic. Nothing of what I say here pretends to have the universal validity of an explanatory theory which establishes dogmas. In many cases it is likely that my explanations, my quotations, and the facts I present, are neither complete nor precise and may even be distorted by my debatable position within the Boom in question: I speak here approximately, tentatively, subjectively, since I prefer my testimony to have more authenticity than rigor. I count myself among those who do not know the fluctuating boundaries of the Boom and I feel unable to fix its hypothetical form, let alone disentangle its content. But whatever may be the position and rank of my work within the history of the contemporary Spanish American novel, my books appeared in and around the 1960s and consequently I feel joined to and defined by the currents and tides of the literary environment of our world, by changes determined with the publication of certain novels that have powerfully influenced my vision and my occupation as a writer. I agree in advance that Salvador Garmendia, for example, or Juan Rulfo or Carlos Martínez Moreno may give very different and even contrary testimony to mine but to give my personal testimony of these works, to say how I experienced them, to recount how I saw these changes happening from my personal point of view and what cast these changes took for me will be, more than anything else, the theme and the purpose of these notes.

2

I BEGAN BY SPEAKING of certain works which "have merited international attention." I did not do it inadvertently, because it seems to me that the most significant changes in the Spanish American novel of recent years are tied to a process of internationalization carried out on various levels.

When I say "internationalization" I am not referring to the eagerness of the publishing houses; nor to the various large monetary prizes; nor to the number of translations by important publishers in Paris, Milan, or New York; nor to the taste for the literary *potin* which now interests a public whose numbers were unsuspected a year ago; nor to the unconcealed interest of magazines and movies and literary agents in all the capitals; nor to the innumerable doctoral dissertations in hundreds of American universities which have as their subject the young—and almost young—writers of Latin America, when previously it was necessary to be at least a name known in the streets before that could happen. Even though no one knows which came first, the chicken or the egg, it seems to me that all these things, positive and stimulating in a rather superficial sense—and always of *much* smaller proportions than those created by the paranoid legend—have been a result of, and not a cause of, the internationalization of the Spanish American novel. Instead of repeating here the series of anecdotes about all these things, it is necessary to speak about something more elusive: about how the Spanish American novel began to speak an international language; about how, in our somewhat provincial environment, when it comes to the novel before the decade of the '60s, the taste and the esthetic values of the writers and the public were changing little by little, until the Spanish American novel came to have the significance it does have and, at the same time, to lead into entertaining, carnivalesque exaggerations.

Before 1960 it was very uncommon to hear laymen speak of the "contemporary Spanish American novel": there were Uruguayan or Ecuadorian, Mexican or Venezuelan novels. The novels of each country were confined within that country's own frontiers and the novels' fame and relevance remained, in most cases, a local affair. "The contemporary Latin American novel" hardly existed outside of anthologies, classrooms, and textbooks—institutions of which the young have always been highly suspicious. The novelist in the Spanish American countries wrote for his parish: about the problems of his parish and in the language of his parish, addressing himself to the number and level of his readers—quite different, certainly, in Paraguay than in Argentina, in Mexico than in Ecuador—which his parish was able to offer him, without much hope of anything else.

For the person who has not lived it, for the young fan accustomed to the fuss that occurs when a fresh Spanish American name appears, for the novice writer who is certain that his manuscript will be snatched up by a half dozen publishers and will at least be read, for the person who has recently entered into all of this, it is impossible to imagine either the isolation in which Spanish American writers found themselves as little as ten years ago or their asphyxiation due to the lack of stimulation and response. Today no one would believe the nearly unsolvable problems which had to be overcome in order to publish a novel, problems which were commonplace in our countries a decade ago.

Not only the high schools, but also the publishing houses, the newspapers, and the timid literary criticism filled us with the European classics from earlier generations as our only models, our necessary points of reference. Angel Rama states that "The great figures project their mastery over very long periods, giving the sensation, from a distance, that in their own countries they have cut the grass at the roots so that nothing new can grow. . . ." It is true: to reprint the works of these "great figures," to praise them, to study them, to teach that one should admire and write novels similar to *Doña Bárbara, Don Segundo Sombra, Brother Ass, The Underdogs, The Vortex,* did not involve any risk, not even any economic risk for the publishers, since it was a question of required reading in the high schools and the universities, and one edition quietly followed another. It seems to me that this monumental omnipresence of the mighty grandfathers engendered, as is often the case, a generation of fathers weakened by their preoccupation with their brief tradition, and we are left without fathers with whom it would please us to identify; fatherless, but, because of that missing link, without a tradition which might enslave us because—and I am speaking most of all of my own experience—our fathers interested us much less than the foreigners.

Perhaps what most stimulates a literary career is for a beginning writer to see the contemporary acquiring form in the pages of another writer; and often contemporary work of poor and dubious quality turns out to be much more inspiring than what is traditional or sacred or of un-doubted, but remote perfection. So, for all the merit we might have been willing to grant these great classic novels, which have remained major attractions for so long, they, and the novels they engendered, seemed alien to us and very distant from our sensibility and our times, located at an immense distance from the brand-new esthetics, de-fined as much by the problems of the modern world as by our indiscriminate reading of these new writers who were dazzling us with their sparks: Sartre and Camus, from whose recent influence we are convalescing; Günther Grass, Moravia, Lampedusa; Durrell, for better or for worse; Robbe-Grillet with all his followers; Salinger, Kerouac, Miller, Frisch, Golding, Capote; the Italians led by Pavese; the English led by the *Angry Young Men* who were just our age and with whom we identified—all of this after we had devotedly devoured "classics" like Joyce,

Proust, Kafka, Thomas Mann, and Faulkner, at least, and had digested them. To reread, at a distance of fifteen years, many of the novelists in the first group who seemed so definitively contemporary to us at that time is to be appalled by the fragility of fleeting literary certainties and to wonder how long the certainty we have today about particular novels of the Boom will last. Still, I think that this risk of a quick death from wanting to express ourselves in forms that embody what is contemporary—something far removed from the exploitations of current topics, a business with which it is often confused—is a very essential part of the literary game, giving it a whole dimension, making it dangerous and attractive—as much for the author as for the perceptive reader. So, with their legacy of vassalage to the Spanish Academy of the Language and to outmoded attitudes toward literature and life, the gentlemen who wrote the basic Spanish American novels—and a large number of their offspring as well—looked to us like statues in a park: some with larger mustaches than others, some with gold chains to their pocket watches and others without, but all essentially indistinguishable and none with any power over us. Neither d'Halmar nor Barrios, neither Mallea nor Alegría offered temptations even remotely like those of Lawrence, Faulkner, Pavese, Camus, Joyce, and Kafka. In the Spanish novel that teachers liked to offer us as an example and, to a certain degree, as something we also might call "our own"—in Azorín, Miró, Baroja, Pérez de Ayala—we discovered stagnancy and poverty when we compared them to their contemporaries in other languages. Perhaps the greatest difference between the novelists of the Boom and their Spanish contemporaries is nothing more than one of time: the earliness with which foreign influences—especially Kafka, Sartre, and Faulkner, without whom the Boom would be impossible to define—flourished in Latin America while the Spaniards lay chained for a much longer time by their own monumental tradition in which not a single link was missing. On the other hand, today's Spanish American novel was from the very beginning a *mestizaje*, a crossbreeding, a disregarding of Hispanic-American tradition (as much disregard for what was Hispanic as for what was American) and draws itself almost totally from other literary sources, because, without a whimper, our orphaned sensibility let itself be infected by the North Americans, the French, the English, and the Italians, all of whom seemed to us more "ours," much more "our own" than a Gallegos or a Güiraldes, for example, or a Baroja.

What the Latin American novel offered us after its classics, those which popular taste and criticism attempted to impose on us as our immediate literary "fathers"—I'm speaking above all of Chile since that is my experience, but I imagine that it cannot have been very different in the other small, poor countries of the continent—were the *criollistas*, who were called *costumbristas* [1] or regionalists in other areas. While the young generation's world was expanding through readings and public appearances which most of all tended to erase the frontiers, the *criollistas*, regionalists, and *costumbristas*, busy as bees, tried on the contrary to reinforce those frontiers between one region

---

[1] *Costumbrista* writers emphasized the "slice of life" of a particular area, attempting to capture with descriptive details the local color and the particularly typical elements of that society. *Criollista* writing, as an extension of this, is a desire to discover what is particularly American, emphasizing especially the landscape and the sociological reality. [G.K.]

and the next, between one country and another, to make them unassailable and hermetic so that our identity, which they evidently viewed as something weak or blurry, would not fade or slip away. With their entomologists' magnifying glasses, they were cataloging the flora and fauna, the tribes and the proverbs which were unmistakably ours. A novel was considered good if it loyally reproduced those autochthonous worlds, all that which specifically makes us different—which separates us—from other areas and other countries of the continent: a type of foolproof, chauvinistic *machismo*.[2] In fact, the work of these *costumbristas*, regionalists, and *criollistas* was very fine and was worthwhile for them. But as that school came to predominate, their canons infected other writers and critics who did not have any reason to adopt these honest though limited aims as their only criteria. And having adopted and spread these views, they defined one of the canons of literary taste that has done the most harm to the Spanish American novel and that is still followed by those who are not very cautious: the only true criterion of excellence is the precision required to depict what is inherently ours, the verifiable verisimilitude that tends to transform a novel into a faithful document portraying or capturing a segment of univocal reality. There were critics in Chile who attempted to explain the failure of Mariano Latorre as a novelist because, as the son of foreigners, he was unable to reproduce the Chilean gambling world exactly. I am not going to limit myself to alleging that this criterion flourished only in Chile. I remember that in 1964 when I read *The Time of*

[2] *Machismo*, which suggests many shades of meaning, mostly connected with the manner in which a man presents himself, here relates to a strong, self-sufficient pose. [G.K.]

the Hero by Mario Vargas Llosa I publicly showed my immediate enthusiasm for that novel; the Peruvian Cultural Attaché in Chile at that time cautioned me not to allow myself to be deceived by a novel which pretended to be a depiction of life in the Miraflores section of Lima. He, who knew the area well, could assure me that the portrayal was inaccurate and so he could prove that the literary merits of *The Time of the Hero* were not as great as the public might think. Literary quality, then, remained subordinate to mimetic and regional criteria.

Along with the *criollistas*, social realism also attempted to raise isolating barriers: the novel of protest, preoccupied with national concerns, with the "important social problems" which urgently needed to be solved, imposed a lasting and deceptive criterion: in addition to being unmistakably ours, as the *criollistas* wanted, the novel should be, above all else, "important," "serious," an instrument which would be directly useful to social progress. Any attitude which might be accused of leaving the bad taste of something that might be labelled "estheticism" was anathema. Formal experimentation was prohibited. The architecture of the novel and its language were to be simple, flat, colorless, sober, and poor. Our rich, native language, naturally baroque, protean, exuberant—and accepted as such in poetry, perhaps because it was already agreed that this was a genre destined for an elite—found itself ironed out by the requirements of the utilitarian novel destined for the masses whose consciousness was to be raised without anything coming between the novel's meaning or its immediate use. The fantastic and the personal elements, the strange or marginal writers, those who "abused" the language or the form, were exiled by these criteria, which

16

reigned for so many years that the magnitude and the potential of the novel were sadly impoverished. In 1962 I tried to convince Zigzag Publishers to reprint the Chilean surrealists Juan Emar and Braulio Arenas, but they refused to do so because these writers were considered odd, only for "specialists." There is no need to be surprised, therefore, that when I also wanted them to reissue Thomas Mann (*Joseph in Egypt*) and Virginia Woolf (*The Waves*), for which Zigzag possessed both the rights and excellent translations, the answer was the same: they were writers for "specialists" and it was not worthwhile to reprint them.

What shackled the novel most was this impoverishing criterion of mimesis and especially mimesis of what was verifiably "ours"—social problems, peoples, landscapes—which was transformed into a measuring stick of literary quality since the quality of a work could be appreciated only by the inhabitants of the country or the region described and was relevant only to them. Since the criterion of practical efficacy and not of literary efficacy came first, those novels which contained so much raw, unpolished novelistic material did not encounter any foreign acceptance or interest, achieving exactly what the regionalist bees wanted: to raise barriers that would separate one country from another, literarily isolating them, praising xenophobia and chauvinism and confusing those concepts with nationalism, more or less transforming the novel into a question of details whose honesty could be discussed only within its own parish because only there would it be of any interest. What was being created in each Spanish American nation, therefore, was a defensive and arrogant Olympus of writers whom we who were younger found unsatisfactory, even though their pressure—more than their influence—weighed on us and on our first novels: these were in most cases the fruits of the struggle between a nationalistic asceticism and the great tides which brought more complex ideas from abroad. We were orphans: but this orphanhood, this position of rejecting what was forced on us as "ours," a position in which we were placed by the novelists who preceded us, produced an emptiness in us, a feeling of not having anything exciting in our own writing; and I do not believe that I am wrong in maintaining that my generation of novelists looked not only (and almost exclusively) outside Latin America but also outside our own language, toward the United States, toward the Anglo-Saxon countries, toward France and Italy, in search of sustenance, opening ourselves up, allowing ourselves to be contaminated by all the "impurities" from the outside: cosmopolitans, snobs, those who introduced foreign customs, those who took up esthetic postures—the new novelists had the aspect of traitors in the naïve gaze of those days. I remember the scandal and shock that was produced in Chile by Jorge Edwards' declaration when he published his first book of short stories, *El patio* (The Patio), stating that he was much more interested in foreign literature and knew it much better than his own. He was the only one of my generation whom I know who dared to speak the truth and to point out a very real situation: in our country—and I suppose in all the nations of Latin America—we find not only that we have almost no one in the immediately preceding generation who can offer us any literary stimulus but also that we encounter a hostile, distrustful attitude when it becomes clear that the new novelists have abandoned the customary path of verifiable, utilitarian, and national reality.

I think that nothing has enriched my generation as much as this lack of our own literary fathers. It gave us a great deal of freedom, and in many ways the emptiness of which I spoke earlier was what permitted the internationalization of the Spanish American novel. The Argentine may postulate Borges as a father, but perhaps he forgets that until a few years ago Borges was the favorite of a very closed cultural and social elite, and that, in general, those who were young then did not share that taste: the awareness of Borges' value came very late—besides occurring suddenly, like many things in our world, after his "discovery" and triumph abroad—so that he had an effect as a father only at the last moment. The recognition of Carpentier in Cuba was also tardy.

At the end of the 1950s, and even more at the beginning of the '60s, the young Spanish American novelists took up a stance which the public did not know whether to define as original or simply as snobbish. When decked out in modernist garlands, literary taste was reduced to a fear of the Spanish Academy of the Language or to a *parti pris* by the vociferating and preaching attitude which accepted only the *machismo* of an "American" language and of autochthonous themes, which never managed to ascertain their own limits. The disfiguring contamination of foreign languages and literatures, the contact with other forms and other arts such as film, painting, or poetry, the inclusion of numerous dialects, forms of slang, and the mannerisms of social groups or specialized sects, the acceptance of the requirements of the fantastic, of the subjective, of the marginal, of emotion, all caused the new novel either to assault the old frontiers or to ignore them, breaking out of its parochial limits: now a Chilean had to write in order to be understood and to be of interest, not only in Talca and Linares but also in Guanajuato and Entrerríos.

I want to add here that it was not that the critics did not suggest European fathers to us. Instead, as is natural, they dedicated themselves primarily to authors who, although in most cases their merit could not be denied, were too distant from the esthetic preoccupations of the youth at that time: Eduardo Mallea, Germán Arciniegas, Agustín Yáñez, Miguel Angel Asturias, Ciro Alegría, Arturo Uslar Pietri. This dedication is explainable—as is the oblivion or at least the relegation which followed—if we realize that the critics who anointed these heroes were generally older and that their literary taste corresponded to that of the preceding generations: the critics tended to praise those who resembled them and who spoke their language, those whose sensibilities and interests corresponded to the established tastes. Which is to say that the critical establishment produced an establishment in the novel. They never mentioned the writers who were *fuori serie*, astonishing, inexplicable, odd, who existed in an obscurer but parallel manner to the anointed of their own generation, but which the critics' silence or myopia concealed from us. One cannot help wondering, a little fearfully, whether the Boom, which today seems so fresh and daring, will in a while be compared by the coming generation to an establishment, one to whom it never occurred that it in fact might be one. Those writers were at least concealed from me: although I was rather curious about the novel, always searching for what was new, I only came to know those novelists ten or fifteen years later: so, I read *Broad and Alien Is the World* in 1946 but *The Lost Steps* in 1957 and Onetti much later; I read *The Bay of Silence* in 1947 but *The Aleph* in 1959. Borges, Carpentier, Onetti were practically unknown in Chile before the 1960s. The exemplary isolation of Onetti delayed the dissemination of his works. The metaphysics and Europeanism of Borges and the excessive language of Carpentier caused them to be labeled, if they were known at all, as esthetes, as writers of useless literature, and they were set aside. On the other hand, Ciro Alegría, Germán Arciniegas, Miguel Angel Asturias, Eduardo Mallea were able to represent the qualities of their continent with dignity, just as the Eminent Victorians had represented the qualities of Imperial England, identifying themselves with the most obvious levels of their country's struggles. These authors were translated into some other languages in their time, but they obtained a very limited circulation.

Since all of these authors occupied the first rank in the narrative at that time and consequently exercised a strong control, none of this would be especially susceptible to criticism if it had not produced the isolation of the younger novelists. In each country, no one knew what was being written in other Latin American countries, especially because it was so difficult to publish a first novel or a first collection of short stories or to get them recognized. All the publishing houses were more or less poor and, in the larger countries, prejudiced in favor of foreign literature, so to overcome the closed circle of the elite in order to get any publisher to take a risk in publishing an unknown name and then, if they managed to do that, to have them print more than a couple of thousand copies destined to accumulate dust in the publishers' cellars without ever leaving the country, was impossible. Rubia Rojas-Paz, with all her influence in the literary world of Buenos Aires, dragged me with my manuscript under my arm to Losada, where they not only did not read me but would not even receive me: they were passionately involved in the publication of Arturo Barea. Our isolation convinced us that this situation was normal, the only one possible. *De mon temps, Monsieur, on n'arrivait pas,* Degas said to a youth who complained of how difficult it was to achieve success. Our situation was that of the nineteenth century, like that of the time of Degas' youth: what predominated was a sense of discouragement, of stasis, of a lack of appreciation for what we were doing, and a certainty that this situation was irreversible, that it was this way because it had always been and would continue to be this way.

I published my first book of short stories, *Veraneo*,[3] in 1955. The Chilean publishing houses, Zigzag, Nascimento, Pacífico, were not interested in my first work because they could not risk publishing an author whose sales were not assured in Chile—in those days people did not think in terms of the Spanish-speaking world. Since I did not have money and because I was not of the age "to ask Father for it," I arranged for ten of my friends to sell ten subscriptions each to my book before it was published and with this ready cash I paid the first installment that Editorial Universitaria demanded of me. My book appeared without a publisher's imprint; a thousand copies with a cover by Carmen Silva. The copies which had been subscribed for were passed out and the heroic campaign

[3] In 1977 Alfred Knopf will publish a translation of Donoso's *Tres novelitas burguesas* under the title *Sacred Families* and David Godine will publish the translation of *El Charleston y otros cuentos* entitled *The Charleston and Other Stories*. [G.K.]

began to sell the rest or to convince bookstore owners to take them, even on consignment. I stood on street corners to offer the book to passing acquaintances while my friends did the same in other sections of the city, until I got enough together to pay the full printing cost. Darío Carmona, in *Ercilla*, was the first to mention my book. Later the critic "Alone" (Hernán Díaz Arrieta),[4] whose weekly literary column in *El Mercurio* was all-powerful at that time, gave me his official praise: he spoke of me and I triumphantly succeeded in selling the thousand copies. I received the Municipal Short Story Prize in 1956. But in spite of translations and anthologies, ten years had to pass before the stories were reprinted.

Nearly all the other Chilean writers of my generation—the so-called Generation of '50 that is said to have been "invented" by Enrique Lafourcade, who was strongly criticized for this "invention," which gave me my first real literary stimulus and a consciousness of what I was able to do—were in the same position as I. Claudio Giaconi, Alfonso Echeverría, Armando Cassígoli, Alejandro Jodorowsky, Luis Alberto Heiremans, María Elena Gertner, Jaime Laso, all of us published books in a rather shameful way, with pleas and pledges, privately or by subscription. Jorge Edwards did it with *El patio* (The Patio) that was sold in Inez Figueroa's store just as my books were, along with pottery from Quinchamali and other handicrafts. Margarita Aguirre published *Cuaderno de una muchacha muda* (A Mute Girl's Notebook) in a rather ephemeral series. I shall never forget Margarita, timid,

[4] Author of *Historia personal de la literatura chilena* [A Personal History of Chilean Literature]. Since I think that the genre of the "personal history" created by him is effective, I have used it in the title of this book.—J.D.

23

ironic, brunette, climbing onto the streetcars of those days with an armful of her thin books and offering them to the passengers who seemed least hostile to her, much as I did with my short stories. That was the measure of our possibilities in the decade of the '50s.

In 1957, when I was looking for a publisher for *Coronation*, and even after I had received the Municipal Prize for my short stories so that occasionally some young writer would recognize me in a bar, Zigzag did not dare to publish it. The editor-in-chief at Zigzag believed that it would be too big an investment for a "difficult book" and therefore a book of unlikely sales—a literary opinion that will help anyone who has read the book to gauge our mentality since it was by no means a *Finnegans Wake*. The directors of Editorial del Pacífico, to whom I also offered *Coronation* since they were writers of my generation, also rejected the novel, advising me to do much pruning, much slicing. Later, Nascimento, the most enterprising publishing house in the country—after Ercilla had been taken over by Zigzag and had lost its individuality—agreed to publish *Coronation*, but under very curious conditions: they would print three thousand copies of which I would receive seven hundred in exchange for giving up my right to an advance and to remainders. I had to sell my seven hundred copies privately and on my own. Then began the second heroic campaign, the distribution of those thick yellow volumes with their cover by Nemesio Antúnez to bookstores which frequently refused to take the book because of distribution agreements with Nascimento. Once again my friends mobilized to sell copies to whomever they could, on the streets, at the university, at parties, in cafes, and I myself went offering the book from house to house. I recall my good-natured father seated at the entrance to the Union Club in a chair covered in Genoan velvet with a stack of yellow volumes at his side, selling them there to his fellow members with their canes, or later at the card table.

The year it was published in Chile, *Coronation* was a "success": it appeared on the last day of 1957. Nevertheless, by considering that three thousand copies were sufficient—and in the end how many more did I expect to sell?—the publishers had to wait several years before reprinting it, and so it stayed out of print. If "everyone" had read it—in Chile, in those years, there still was an "everyone"—why bother to reprint it? That would be done when it was named a scholarly or university text, an event still a long way off. Nor did anyone ever think of distributing and selling it in other countries. It was this way with almost all the novels of that time. The impressarios of publishing and distributing neither imported nor exported while the immense Spanish-speaking world was consumed with hunger, convinced of its inability to produce its own sustenance. At the end of the '50s, there was no consciousness of those millions of possible readers or of those hundreds of young writers eager to communicate, and, at the start, the first novels by the best people of my generation—Mario Benedetti, for example, Augusto Roa Bastos, myself, Carlos Martínez Moreno—stayed locked within their national boundaries: it was impossible to buy novels of foreign writers in our country, and at the same time it was impossible to export our own books. They said that it was all to keep foreign currency within the country, but there was more than enough currency to import Walt Disney comic books.

Mysteriously, however, some copies of our works were

slipping out. Suddenly a letter: someone who had read one of the books in Cuba or in Montevideo. How did these books travel? How would the yellow copy of *Coronation*, which the bibliophile Franco Cerutti bought, arrive at a used bookstore in Managua, Nicaragua? Fernando Tola found another yellow copy of *Coronation* in a bargain bookstore of Barcelona in 1970 and the bookseller asked him for fifty pesetas. Tola did not have the money with him at that moment, and a month later—after the appearance of *The Obscene Bird of Night*—the price had risen to 400 pesetas. Another copy reached someone who would later become my great friend, Beatriz Guido, who commented upon meeting a certain Chilean painter at a swimming pool in Buenos Aires that she could not understand why there was so much talk about *Coronation*, it was such a mediocre novel . . . that painter answered that the author was her boy friend; Beatriz Guido immediately took a refreshing dip in the pool. Paco Giner de los Ríos bought two copies of *Coronation* from Juanita Eyzaguirre in Santiago, one for himself and the other for his brother-in-law, Joaquín Díez-Canedo; Carlos Fuentes saw the book for the first time in Díez-Canedo's library, but he was not able to read it because Díez-Canedo said he would not loan him the bulky book: it was an interesting book but very difficult to obtain.

Consequently, that was our destiny: to publish on our own, to sell against all odds, and in the best of cases, as in that of *Coronation*, to be well-received by local critics and to have a feature article by "Alone" in *El Mercurio* devoted to our work. So one entered on the lowest rung of the nation's glories, destined, perhaps, for the Academy of the Language, and, with luck, for the diplomatic corps: that was what was called "the career of letters." That, and perhaps being recognized by some aspiring writer on a bus or drinking wine some nights at Bosco with friends who have now disappeared, or being invited from time to time to the gatherings at Lolito Echeverría's home to rub elbows with the "greats" and to wait patiently for some unusual circumstance to stimulate us sufficiently so that we would not be afraid to write a second novel, and so climb up another rung on the difficult ladder of the national Olympus where it was impossible to skip a step because everything was stratified.

When "Alone" brought me to Marta Brunet's home, she said to me: "I still haven't read your novel, but it's of great interest to me because they tell me that you carry on the great tradition of Chilean realism." The words of Marta Brunet, who thirty years before had been "launched" by "Alone," frightened me. They made me understand how limited the Chilean literary appreciation of that time could be, when not even the most informed reader, able to perceive a thousand nuances in contemporary European novels, would make the effort to understand something other than the layer of "faithfully depicted reality" within the world of ambiguous allusions which a novel is. Undoubtedly, it was a well-intentioned environment with one or two voices capable of pointing out different things that generally got resolved in a very personalized, newspaper-controversy sort of tattle, but it was essentially an environment with little room or tolerance for contradictory or apparently marginal literary attitudes, a world without any variety of taste or possibility. Hence, Chilean criticism was nearly unanimous in praising the "reality" in which I depicted "the decadence of the upper class," since for a large part of my readers that was my goal, my purpose, and my intention. With the few exceptions of those who have noticed something beyond the surface of my books, Chilean criticism has continued to praise the same layer of realism that it praised in my first novel, although in more recent works the plane of reality may be reduced to a minimum and the "critical intention" may be nonexistent.

They also praised the naturalness and spontaneity of the light style, a style which was transparent in this first novel and which did not come between the author and the reader. They praised what was naturally verifiable, which in *Coronation* was everything: the familiar, the quotidian, the creditable, the dialogues which reproduced with an "almost photographic" simplicity the speech of different social classes, everything so simple, so natural, except, of course, that last ugly and ridiculous scene which did not please many people and which was generally considered an exaggeration of bad taste that González Vera, for example, would never have committed: it was imperative to conform strictly to classic proportions. After reading the first part of *Coronation*, which is really very simple and natural, a distinguished woman telephoned Manuel Rojas to tell him: "I'm reading the best novel that has been written in Chile." Several days later, having gotten into the second part and especially after reaching the end, she called him again and told him: "I was wrong. It isn't the best Chilean novel as it seemed it was going to be." The liberty of the last scene, the episode in Omsk, made her consider it "pretentious," not very simple, and for Chilean taste there is no anathema worse than not being "simple."

Despite the fact that a large part of *Coronation* was written under the pressure of those many canons of simplicity, verisimilitude, social criticism, and irony, which make it fall into a type of intimist novel, very characteristically Chilean, by that time I already had an idea that those qualities of national taste were not the only yardstick with which to measure excellence; that, on the contrary, the baroque, the distorted, the excessive could all increase the possibilities of the novel.

When I was in Isla Negra in 1957 finishing *Coronation*, the musician Juan Orrego Salas returned from Caracas with news of a great novel which, as he told it, had been written by a musicologist and which was having a great deal of repercussion in the Caribbean area: *The Lost Steps* by Alejo Carpentier. I devoured that novel in one enormous bite, reading night and day without stopping and then I reread it while I reworked my own novel. Perhaps, although in a very remote way, this admirable opposition to the measure of taste which had confined me may have made possible the modest freedom with which I treated the last part of *Coronation*, whose style seemed to fall, at that time, so far outside Chilean taste. I think that perching on top of *The Lost Steps* I was able for the first time to look beyond the barriers of simplicity and realism as our literature's sole destiny. I had been pleased that it was not the destiny of other literatures, but now I was on my own ground—in order to observe not only a much greater amplitude but also dimensions not totally out of reach.

Asphyxiated in my Chilean surroundings, dissatisfied with the limitations placed upon me, six months after *Coronation* appeared and without a nickel in my pocket, I decided to begin a tour of America with the purpose of learning what was happening outside of my country. I got together some money to pay for my trans-Andean train

29

passage to Buenos Aires, and there Raquel Lyon de Maza—wife of the ambassador from Chile—arranged to have the Argentine Society of Writers house me free of charge in a half-demolished room in the rear part of the Society's rambling colonial house, while I searched for and found work. It was in this tiny room that I read Borges for the first time, and I was overwhelmed: under his immediate influence I wrote a horrendous short story—that has nothing to do with Borges and which I have never included in any of the anthologies of my "complete" stories—and I sold it to *Américas* magazine for seventy-five dollars, which came at just the right time for me in my precarious situation. I dedicated it to that Chilean painter who had caused Beatriz Guido's plunge into the pool and whom I married much later. I met Pepe Bianco whose intelligence seemed to me not only prodigious but of a sort totally different from everything being produced on the other side of the mountains; Elvira Orphée who, inconceivably and magically, was a personal friend of Italo Calvino and Elsa Morante, two writers whom I admired; Augusto Roa Bastos, alone and in exile; writers of the extreme left who came to the home of Bernardo Kordon and his Chilean wife; Catholic writers of the magazine *Señales*. Perhaps none of this was necessarily "better" than what Chile offered; but it was different, and that was important to me at that time, that change of perspective.

One unforgettable afternoon Pipina Moreno Hueyo de Diehl Ayereza (the rosary of last names is necessary to identify a *porteño* of good stock) brought Borges and me to meet the great-granddaughters—or great-grand-nieces—of Jose Hernández, enchanting elderly spinsters, most likely teachers, who lived modestly in the Belgrano section of the city. It was rumored in Buenos Aires that one of these ladies was a medium and was in communication with the author of *Martín Fierro*, which delighted Borges. The five of us sat around a table covered with a cloth embroidered with flowers by one of these women, illuminated by a low light which isolated each of us within its beams and its silence. With our hands on the table we awaited the mystical moment in which Hernández would somehow show himself. But he remained mute. While we waited transfixed, the slow, hesitating voice of Jorge Luis Borges began to recite stanzas of *Martín Fierro*—including several variants he knew—as if his blind eyes were seeing Hernández, tall and long-haired, who had appeared in the room in order to give to Borges poems which life had not given him time to execute. But it was useless. Hernández neither spoke nor appeared and his descendants offered us such a very sweet wine, with even sweeter pastries, that we were forced to leave hurriedly.

I read, enthusiastically and indiscriminately, a great deal of everything during the two years I stayed there. I read Dalmiro Sáenz, Roberto Arlt (the anti-Borgesian writers had taken possession of him; the Borgesians still had not discovered Macedonio Fernández to counter the attack), Norah Lange, David Viñas, the first novel of Sarita Gallardo, Ernesto Sábato's *The Tunnel*, novels of all sorts as long as they were recently published, novels written in English by elegant women in hats, novels of muscular, virile writers who thought they had invented both knife fights and the tango, Murena, those in Victoria Ocampo's school, Bioy Casares, Silvina Bullrich, Mújica Laínez, Manauta . . . an interminable number of people, an interminable number of recent new novels, of immensely varying quality, obeying antagonistic tastes or slogans, talked about at noisy dinners at the Edelweiss with photographers, painters, psychoanalysts, or at intimate dinners at the "Adam" just before catching the last train to Belgrano. I spent some time at Margarita Aguirre's ranch—she has been my friend all my life and at that time she was married to an Argentine gentleman—writing a series of stories, most of which were failures except those that later appeared in *The Charleston*. Rosa Chacel came to know *Coronation* from the pages of *SUR*. I had evaded jail, and although I returned to live in Chile, I think that after this trip to Buenos Aires my literary vision changed definitively.

I am very familiar with the disdain with which intellectuals regard literary congresses, poetry contests, roundtable discussions, meetings, and similar activities, all of which are a little underdeveloped. But for me they have always been stimulating and productive—ever since those first unforgettable conferences on the short story where Enrique Lafourcade launched the Generation of '50—so I hope God will prevent me from having that well-known, blasé attitude toward them. In our underdeveloped world—it still was not "the developing world" or "the third world"—it was necessary to seize every stimulus in order not to become stagnant. Hence, I would like to situate the growth of my awareness of what was happening and of what would happen to the Latin American novel in my sudden change of perspective due to my stay in Buenos Aires (1958–1960), which would culminate and be clarified in the Congress of Intellectuals at the University of Concepción, Chile, in 1962, in which Pablo Neruda, José María Arguedas, José Miguel Oviedo,

Augusto Roa Bastos, Pepe Bianco, Carlos Fuentes, Claribel Alegría, Alejo Carpentier (all without a Nobel Prize), professors, goldsmiths, painters, and a full team of Chilean writers participated. It was very international and modern—with simultaneous interpreters and all the rest—a sort of huge intellectual carnival, with picnics, dips in the ocean, exhibitions, flirting, and meals. There were many varied themes during the working sessions, and the speeches fluctuated in quality between the most innocuous and the brilliance of Pepe Bianco's paper. But I would like to emphasize here—and this is why I even mention this Congress of Intellectuals—that the theme which was repeated and repeated and which clearly predominated was the common complaint that as Latin Americans we knew European and North American literature perfectly, in addition to our own national literatures, but that isolated by a lack of means and by the egotism and the myopia of the publishing houses and the very methods of book distribution, we were almost completely ignorant of literature from other countries on the continent. What we talked about most was the isolation of the writer in our midst and his lack of cultural contact: I remember the spectacular embrace, during the debates, of Thiago de Melo, wearing a long red poncho, and José María Arguedas, answering him in Quechua, surrounded by the audience's applause, in order to obtain a closeness which was not achieved by means of literature. We spoke of organizing conferences and colloquia, of founding publishing houses which would publish everything worthwhile that appeared on the continent, we planned magazines and book distribution: all of this, of course, starting from the assumption that nothing could be organized according to commercial standards, not

33

only because what is commercial always carries connotations of impurity but also because nothing seemed more impossible to us than that there would be a real demand for what we produced. We all were certain that none of this would function if it were not subsidized by someone or something . . . We harshly discussed our short-sighted critics who did not dare to spread the new values. There was a common complaint that in the bookstores of Bogotá, or of Santiago, for example, it was very easy to obtain a copy of Mauriac or of Steinbeck, but it was nearly impossible to find something by Arguedas or Fuentes: in short, we were discovering our ammunition but the ammunition was to discover it. Especially if I add here, as a curious comment, that during the Congress of Intellectuals in Concepción in 1962, the names of Sábato, Cortázar, Borges, Onetti, García Márquez, Vargas Llosa (he published his first novel that year), and even Rulfo, were hardly mentioned. If they were, it was so passingly that I have forgotten. In 1962 they were nearly unknown or marginal. The Boom had not yet begun.

From today's perspective, not only does the protest against isolation and the lack of diffusion which dominated that Congress seem incredible, but similarly the fact that some of the works later recognized as basic or determining constituents of the Boom (if the Boom does exist), several novels by Onetti, stories by Borges and Cortázar, *Pedro Páramo* and *The Burning Plain*, and the first things by García Márquez had already been published. The truth was that it was impossible to acquire these works outside of their respective countries, that prizes and national quarrels distorted a more universal perspective, so that very few people had ever heard of these authors whose works re-

34

mained imprisoned within a small sect or within geographic boundaries.

It is superfluous to say that absolutely none of the initiatives proposed and discussed during the Congress of Intellectuals in Concepción in 1962 was acted upon. But in my own experience, at least, the Congress traced a very clear line, one which allowed me to dare to stop thinking literarily of what is "ours" only in so far as Chile was concerned; and, instead, to start thinking that what is "ours"—what is mine and what is Chilean—could, and had to, interest millions and millions of Spanish-speaking readers, and by breaking with such clearly marked boundaries, could invent a fuller and more international language.

3

LOOKING, AS ALWAYS, at the phenomenon from my personal point of view, I see the Mexican Carlos Fuentes as the first active and conscious agent of the internationalization of the Spanish American novel of the 1960s. He offered me a new angle of vision and also a need to make it mine—as much in what is strictly literary as in more profane areas.

A year before the Congress of Intellectuals in Concepción, a novel called *Where the Air Is Clear* by Fuentes had fallen into my hands. As I read it, literature took on another dimension, because the book brusquely tore me away from the esthetic to which, despite Buenos Aires, I was still attached. So much so that on a purely personal level I think that it was this trauma—uprooting me from my homespun esthetic in order to plant me within a broader esthetic—that left me incapable of finishing *The Obscene Bird of Night*, which by then was conceived and perhaps even begun. Incapable, simply because I was afraid of not being able to live up to the literary demands then suggested to me as so superior to the ones I had come to think of as my own.

It is possible that *Where the Air Is Clear* is not Carlos Fuentes' best novel. *The Death of Artemio Cruz, Aura*, and the later novels have changed the perspective with which I look back on his first novel. But besides its infinite qualities—the famous ambition to encompass everything, for example, and the lyrical force which distinguish his work—it is necessary to note that it belongs to a group of profoundly Latin American books: the line of those which take over the task of digging below the surface of our cities and our countries in order to unearth their essence, their soul. What does it mean to be Mexican? Peruvian? Argentine? Today very few writers bother to ask themselves what it means to be English, French, or Italian; and if they do, very few non-specialists give any importance to their books. The age-old cultural traditions of these latter peoples, with their successive load of affirmations and negations forming an uninterrupted chain, answer that question with varying attempts at epic, lyric, and pastoral poems, with novels, with philosophical systems, with essays, and with short stories. But in the recently born countries of our American world, in countries lacking their own body of culture, whose dialectic, through the centuries, would have been sketching their clear physiognomies in terms and forms understandable to contemporary western culture, there are a series of books aspiring to serve as shortcuts for reaching, as quickly as possible, a consciousness of what is national in each of the countries. I am referring to books from very distinct literary categories like *X-Ray of the Pampa* by Ezequiel Martínez Estrada, *Chile o una loca geografía* (Chile or A Crazy Geography) by Benjamín Subercaseaux, *Labyrinth of Solitude* by Octavio Paz, and *Lima la horrible* (Lima the Horrible) by Sebastián Salazar Bondy. The attitude revealed in these books—their anguished, adolescent curiosity to see themselves naked in the mirror in order to know themselves once and for all and to be able to grow—developed from the essay to imaginative literature converted into works such as *Montevideanos* (Montevideans) by Mario Benedetti and Leopoldo Marechal's *Adán Buenosayres*, *La bahía de silencio* (The Bay of Silence) and *La pasión de Juan Argentino* (The Passion of Juan Argentino) by Eduardo Mallea, and Carlos Fuentes' *Where the Air Is Clear*—the most interesting and complex of all, the most pertinent, the one that completes the circle.

When *Where the Air Is Clear* appeared in translation, its North American critics pointed out that it was easy to find influences of John Dos Passos' *Manhattan Transfer* and the *U.S.A.* trilogy in it. Although the kinship may be evident on a certain level, I believe that Dos Passos' documentary coldness, his dogmatic certainty that there is a univocal reality determined by social forces and that it is sufficient to focus on it with the eye of the camera in order to write a good novel, place Carlos Fuentes' work, with its unbridled lyricism, and Dos Passos' work at opposite poles.

Perhaps the greatest amazement that the reading of *Where the Air Is Clear* provoked in me was Fuentes' denial,

39

precisely, of a univocal Mexican reality, his rejection—and his literary use—of the spurious, of appearances. His attitude was not one of documentation, like that of the novelists who surrounded me, but rather one of investigation. And the excellence of *Where the Air Is Clear* was that the investigation had nothing of the discursive about it but, on the contrary, was deeply embedded in the body of the novel itself. Mario Vargas Llosa's definition of the writer as an exorcist of his own demons is useful inasmuch as the author does not know these demons when he begins to write and is therefore incapable of postulating them; but he can commit the magical act—for that reason the word "exorcise"—of using his own self, implacably determined to invent a language, to invent a form whose goal is the bringing about of the sorcerer's act of creating a literature which clarifies nothing, which does not explain but which is itself question and answer, the inquiry and the outcome, the executioner and the victim, the disguise and the unmasked. In relation to this, it is true that Carlos Fuentes' gaze in *Where the Air Is Clear* is directed outward, toward society and its problems, toward history and anthropology; but on the other hand, in an existential adventure of the author in search of himself, he also looks toward the individual who is looking and writing and at the same time criticizing his own looking and writing. The great difference between Carlos Fuentes and John Dos Passos is the Mexican's break with realism, and if I found myself hard pressed to compare *Where the Air Is Clear* with a novel by some North American, I would most likely choose— for his exaltation of the lyrical self which grants deformity, ambiguity, and heat to those novels which otherwise would lay anchored in realism—Thomas Wolfe and his disordered quartet which culminates in *You Can't Go Home Again*. It is language, uncovered by the elevated novelistic temperature conferred by an exaggerated self, which takes over the role of the protagonist. And for this very reason I cannot compare Fuentes' book, as has been done, to the German novels from between the wars: neither to *The Devils* by Heimito von Doderer nor to *The Sleepwalkers* by Herman Broch, nor to Thomas Mann's *Buddenbrooks*, nor to *The Man Without Qualities* by Robert Musil, which I realize Fuentes knows and admires . . . or admired. Those authors are intellectuals who postulate their demons before they begin to write. In *Where the Air Is Clear*, on the other hand, Fuentes takes delight in the pleasure of sensing the demons prowling around, confuses himself with them, and far from postulating them, he asks, sometimes shouting, what their names are.

Not only does Fuentes use many different and at times contradictory means of writing novels, not only does he try unlikely tricks which give him, on a certain level, an aspect of disordered eclecticism and on another produce a variety of textures and of velocities and rhythms of movement, but he also entrusts his imperative choice of form to language. The important thing about the lyrical self that serves here as a unifying language is its power to transform things until even the anthropological fact is incorporated into poetry; his alternating artificiality and naturalness become investigations into what is artificiality and naturalness; his freedom to absorb anglicisms, barbarisms, indigenous or idiotic elements and neologisms, transforms illegitimacy and *mestizaje* into the central theme of the book realized at the level of language; his subjective and shamelessly eloquent lyricism embodies his capacity for

41

cruelty and satire, for passing from a psychologically credible human being to the puppet and the masses.

When I began to read *Where the Air Is Clear*, this overloaded and baroque lyricism almost made me feel a little embarrassed, as if someone were undressing in public: in Chile, an ordered and ironic country, where only Neruda had licence—and perhaps a true capacity—to execute lyrical flights which would not cause people to laugh in a few years, the unbridled lyricism seemed to be reserved for aging, tropical, female poets who had suffered a great deal and confused their sighs with their poetic prose: in general, it was considered a pretentious and vulgar cliché. But right here is where Carlos Fuentes presented me with a virile and personal lyricism, filled with obscenities, redundancies, and barbarisms which, far from lifting the last veil off a deliquescent soul, was the literary flag which took possession of our baroque American impurity in a powerful attempt at synthesis.

The Chilean dogma of the need for a transparent and pure language that, in the manner of Nicanor Parra, embodies our irony was the first thing that fell apart as I read Carlos Fuentes' novel. It is true that I had read Joyce, Lawrence, Faulkner, and Thomas Wolfe and therefore knew that many things can be done with language, that the sightlines of a novel do not have to be circumscribed within Tolstoy's if one is not Tolstoy: "Describe your village and you will describe the world" was almost the only dogma that, poorly understood, was applied in Chile. But Carlos Fuentes, a man more or less my own age, a Latin American, a man quite similar and very much a counterpart to me, determined by circumstances rather close to mine, dared to overturn this sacred dogma.

But the fact that Carlos Fuentes' lyricism might have been leading to a search, to a synthesis desired but never formulated, or rather formulated in a hundred contradictory ways, meant that the intellectual element had great importance in his novel. And this intellectual element—comparable in my literary world to "cold," "disdainful," "aristocratic," but never to "intelligent"—was as forbidden as lyricism was in the Chilean novel of my time. To say that there was an important intellectual component in a novel was an anathema which allowed it to be branded immediately as pretentious. And in Chile, a poor, proud, egalitarian, legalistic country, the greatest sin is to seem pretentious, just as the greatest virtue is simplicity.

Nevertheless, *Where the Air Is Clear,* which was lyrical and intellectual, was not pretentious; rather, it was ambitious, which is quite different: it did not present the microcosm of the Tolstoy village as described by one of its inhabitants; but, on the contrary, presented a conception of the world which encompassed all social classes; the Mexican panorama in its present and its past and in its myths and struggles; its present born from the conflict between the Spaniards and the Indians, between the mestizo and the Yankee, between the Catholic priest dressed in black and the splendid priests of the old bloody and autochthonous religions; it was the anthropology and knowledge of the politics of yesterday and today studying the survival of the 365 churches in Cholula constructed on top of 365 Aztec sanctuaries, and their relationship to popular music as well as to color, races, revolutions, agriculture, heroes, traitors . . . a synthesis not developed before the writer sat down to write, as had been done up until then, but developed right there on the page itself; it included ev-

43

erything in a motley fresco that often seemed disconnected because it did not obey the accepted rules of composition. *Unity* within the novel had been a sacred concept for me: I remember that among those of my generation in Chile, the greatest words of praise were to say that such and such a novel was "round" or "closed." (The news had not yet arrived that Umberto Eco had published *Opera aperta*.) But this admirable novel by Carlos Fuentes had nothing of the closed or simple about it, nothing of the documentary. It was, on the contrary, a synthesis including all the illegitimacies of race and taste and language and form where artificiality dominated naturalness and imagination subjugated realism, obeying a powerful, personal viewpoint rather than any pre-novelistic unities.

Reading *Where the Air Is Clear* was a cataclysm for me. Until then, I had been governed by a paralyzing good taste, and, for me, the politics and forces giving shape to our history were a matter of home-town gossip on the level of friendly phone calls, never on the level of myths, invasions, or idolatries. No, Chile's political failure in 1962 could not have looked to anyone like a question of private visions of the world or of disordered lyricism; it was a question of phone calls to find out if it were really true that so-and-so had stolen such-and-such a number of millions in such-and-such shady deal, or who was sleeping with whom, or who had associated with whom as a result of last summer's vacation: a world of satire and vaudeville much like the novel of manners—perhaps this was the reason for the popularity of the Chilean novel of daily life—and much like the *roman à clef* in which everyone recognized the characters strolling down Ahumada Avenue or having an aperitif in the Carrera or the Crillon.

44

It was clear that the mold of the novel such as I knew it and, above all, such as I felt to be within my grasp would no longer be able to serve me after I read *Where the Air Is Clear*. Even the revelation I had reading *The Lost Steps* stopped seeming so intense to me. I realized that that novel by Carpentier, seductive and extremely rich as it had seemed to me when I read it, was insufficient, did not belong to the scope outlined by Carlos Fuentes even though Carpentier's influence could be noticed in Fuentes. In some way, in *The Lost Steps* all the rules of the old novelistic game were still in force: unity reigned, and the narration—that scaffolding which must be destroyed in order to uncover the lines of the literary edifice—continued to have primacy, without being subordinated, as it is in *Where the Air Is Clear*, to the continual bombardment of inquiry as to other possibilities of writing. Most of all, Carpentier's overwhelmingly adorned language remained a question of "style" and did not truly break with anything that preceded it; rather, it was the re-vision of eternal rhetoric through a very personal magnifying glass, but it never truly moved away from the modernism of Valle-Inclán. This was absolutely *not* what Carlos Fuentes was doing, since his language could not be reduced to problems of "style," and, in its audacity and its novelty, his attempt surpassed, it seems to me, all of Alejo Carpentier's work.

This awareness that someone in my world and of my generation had written a novel of such formal freedom that it had exploded all my laws was the first real stimulus that I, as a writer, received from another writer. My voracious reading of novels from all over the world, my study in some depth of writers like Henry James (a taste acquired at Princeton and never abandoned), Marcel Proust, and

Faulkner, contributed an enthusiasm and a certain measure of technical skill, of theory; but these authors always exercised an influence at the level of knowledge: they did not invade my world, they did not harmonize with me to the extent that in competing with them I would be trying to emulate them. My reading of *Where the Air Is Clear* was completely to the contrary: that novel was a vital impulse, a fierce incentive to my life as a writer, a spur to my envy, to the need to emulate, which mixed with my astonishment and my admiration to air out my closed-up house. Perhaps my temperamental Chilean character, critical and ironic, perhaps my having grown accustomed to a certain scope, allowed me to see clearly that it would be absurd to attempt a Chilean version of *Where the Air Is Clear*, since my national world, or at least my vision and understanding of that world, did not lend itself to that. On the other hand, my enthusiasm in reading this novel did not prevent me from realizing that it was related to the howling murals of Rivera, Orozco, and Siqueiros in a certain pedagogical orientation, which, in its weakest moments, moves toward the foreground and dangerously threatens to transform everything into an allegory more determined to point at things outside the novel than within the novel itself.

In 1962 it was announced in the Chilean press that Carlos Fuentes would be attending the Congress of Intellectuals at the University of Concepción. It seemed incredible to me that I, also invited to participate in that event along with a legion of Chilean writers, was going to have the opportunity to meet him. I lost a little of my natural reticence and, checking the time of his plane's arrival, just like any fan, I put my copy of *Where the Air Is Clear* under my arm to take it to the airport so that the author could sign it. Seeing him come off the plane, I approached to ask for his autograph. Fernando Alegría, who came from his university in the United States to participate in this Congress, introduced me to Fuentes, who said to me:

"You're Pepe Donoso?"

". . ."

"You don't remember, but we were in school together, at the Grange, when my father was a diplomat here in Santiago: I was several grades below you so you don't remember me. I saw *Coronation* at Joaquín Díez-Canedo's home, but I've only paged through it. I'm very interested in reading it, but I haven't been able to get a copy. You'll have to give me one."

We became friends. He spoke English and French perfectly. He had read every novel—including Henry James, whose name still did not mean anything in the solitary regions of South America—and he had seen all the paintings and all the films in all the capitals of the world. He did not have the annoying arrogance of pretending to be a simple son of the people, as was more or less the fashion among Chilean intellectuals at that time; he assumed his role of individual and intellectual with ease, uniting the political with the social and the esthetic, and being, moreover, an elegant and refined person who was not afraid to look it. I remember in that Congress of Intellectuals at Concepción when he went to the podium to speak, the two little daughters of Ester Matte-Alessandri, who could not have been more than seven and eight and were seated right in front of me, did not stop talking, in rather loud voices, about how handsome he seemed to them—which prevented me from hearing the first part of Fuentes' paper.

47

He was elegantly dressed and it was easy to see that his clothes were important to him: you must remember that I am speaking of a pre-Carnaby Street, pre-mod era when a man, not to mention a Latin American intellectual, was not able to give, must not have given any importance to something as frivolous and bourgeois as elegance or imagination or boldness in attire. Especially if the man were in Fuentes' political position, this frivolity was obviously irreconcilable with the high and difficult mission he would have to discharge. But despite his elegance, it turned out that Carlos Fuentes had very vigorous missions, perhaps more vigorous than those of anyone else there.

The other intellectuals traveled from Santiago to Concepción on a specially chartered plane. But Fuentes is as afraid of flying as I am, while, on the other hand, we like trains very much—memories of old Sherlock Holmes and Marlene Dietrich movies—and we always take them if the opportunity presents itself. So we went to Concepción by train, he, my wife, and I, together making that long journey which allowed me to become well-acquainted with the author of *Where the Air Is Clear* and to realize with which parts of him I could and could not identify.

In this sense, the most important thing that Carlos Fuentes told me during the trip to Concepción was that after the Cuban Revolution he agreed to speak publicly only of politics, never of literature; that in Latin America the two were inseparable and that now Latin America could look only toward Cuba. His enthusiasm for the figure of Fidel Castro in that period and his faith in the revolution excited the entire Congress of Intellectuals, which was strongly politicized as a result of his presence. The large number of writers from all the countries on the continent almost unanimously demonstrated their support for the Cuban cause. I think that this faith and political unanimity—or near unanimity—was then, and continued to be until the Padilla case exploded in 1971,[1] one of the major factors in the internationalization of the Latin American novel, unifying outlooks and goals, providing an ideological structure to which one could be more or less close—seldom totally opposed—and for a time giving the feeling of a continental cohesion. A large variety of attitudes toward the Cuban Revolution had existed among the writers, ranging from my own congenital political indifference in which, as much as I try to the contrary, my feeling always remains critical—I feel this limitation as Borges perhaps must feel his blindness—to the total commitment of Carlos Fuentes and, later, of Vargas Llosa. Some attitudes have changed with the years: Guillermo Cabrera Infante, a Cuban diplomat who at the beginning was unconditionally in favor of the revolution, became a critic and later a denouncer; and the position of Julio Cortázar who from a passive sympathizer came to be a very active one. And just as I experienced for the first time at the Congress of Intellectuals in Concepción that sudden and powerful tide of sympathy for a political cause which was unifying the continent and all its writers, so the Padilla case marked an end to that unity by sacrificing the loyalties and the work of an entire decade, dissolving that fantasy of not

[1] In 1968 the Unión de Escritores y Artistas de Cuba (UNEAC) presented awards to a play by Anton Arrufat and to a collection of poems by Heberto Padilla. Both works were considered counterrevolutionary, and Padilla was subsequently arrested on March 20, 1971. He was not released until April 27. His arrest began a long debate throughout Latin America on intellectual freedom and the failures of the Cuban regime. [G.K.]

49

being relegated to our little national fights, as was the case before 1960. I think that if the Boom had nearly complete unity in anything—accepting the variety of shadings—it was in the faith in the cause of the Cuban Revolution; I think the disillusionment produced by the Padilla case destroyed that faith and destroyed the unity of the Boom.

Without a doubt, it was Pablo Neruda and Carlos Fuentes who set the tone for that, to me, historic Congress of Intellectuals in Concepción. The enthusiasm and the faith in Cuba were so strong at that moment that, between the Chilean and the Mexican, they convinced Alejo Carpentier—who, contrary to the high-sounding statements of the others, defined himself as "a student of literature and music"—that he should not read his prepared paper, "Magical Elements in Caribbean Literature," but in its place should improvise some dull thing on Fidel Castro's educational reforms which then seemed more pertinent. In an open stadium next to a waterfall, if I remember correctly, Pablo Neruda, dressed in a brilliant black silk shirt brought from China, read lines dedicated to the beauty of Matilde, his wife, and to Cuba. Nilda Núñez del Prado, Guayasamín, Pepe Bianco, Chilean writers, poets from everywhere, each one took a position in regard to Cuba, if not in public then certainly in private. And in a battle of memorable violence, when Frank Tannenbaum, Professor of Latin American History at Columbia University, attempted to describe the insignificant number of protectionist and picturesque relations that the United States maintained with Cuba and Latin America, Carlos Fuentes swept him from the dais with a brilliant speech bristling with facts, dates, statistics, production figures, quotations from public documents and private conversations, that definitively proved the United States' policy of intervention and abuse in Latin America and left the North American stammering and ashamed in the midst of the audience's laughter. When the Congress of Intellectuals broke up in Santiago, the literary temperature had greatly changed and risen, the rules and the audience were going to be different and we were going to determine them ourselves.

Fuentes asked me to give him *Coronation* so that he could take it with him. Delighted, I did so. Nevertheless, during the year following the Congress of Intellectuals and in spite of a pleasant but not very extensive correspondence with Fuentes, my enthusiasm in regard to the realization of all that the Congress had suggested to me was growing cold. I felt that they were moving ahead, publishing novels which were too big and brilliant and that I was lagging behind: *The Death of Artemio Cruz* appeared and Fuentes dazzled me again; I read *Sobre héroes y tumbas* (About Heroes and Tombs) with which Sábato triumphantly came out of the drought his enemies in Buenos Aires had predicted would last forever; I read *The Winners* and in the following year *Hopscotch* by Julio Cortázar, known as a short-story writer to whom an altar of admiration was raised in Eduardo Jonquieres' home in Belgrano and in very few other places. Nevertheless, I received a very generous letter from Carlos Fuentes in which he expressed his enthusiasm for my novel: "I find it absurd that this is not better known and has not been translated. Send it to my literary agent in New York, Carl D. Brandt, and I'll write him to see what he can do for it."

Fuentes' admiration delighted and stimulated me. Just as during our trip to Concepción he had told me that he wanted to write a Balzacian trilogy beginning with *The*

Good Conscience, I told him of the nucleus of what years later would be transformed into *The Obscene Bird of Night*. Despite the lack of boldness in *Coronation*, its everyday quality, an offshoot of the classic *costumbrismo* of our environment, the exchange of plans made me feel to a certain degree comparable to Carlos Fuentes. But . . . this talk of translations . . . of literary agents in New York . . . well, those were out of proportion, unthinkable things, things for Fuentes, with his confidence and certainty in himself, with his friendship with Fidel Castro, things appropriate, it seemed to me then, to someone who had the world at his fingertips and was running it. . . . No, Fuentes was wrong, those things did not happen to Chilean writers, could not happen to me, who, after all, had only written one novel about my grandmother with arteriosclerosis and her equally arteriosclerotic servants and about a friend's uncle in Chile, the most remote and at that time the most stagnant country of the continent. In spite of my wife's urgings, I did not do what Fuentes asked: send copies to Carl Brandt in New York, and to English, Polish, and Russian critics. I did nothing. What Fuentes was reaching for was impossible.

But without my knowing it, my wife, who at that time was working at the cultural bureau of the Brazilian Embassy, made up packages of the fat yellow books on her own account and hidden from me. Spending the week's fuel budget on airmail postage, she mailed I have no idea how many copies. So that when Carlos Fuentes called me several months later from Mexico—I can still hear his voice: "Congratulations. Alfred Knopf, the most important gringo publishing house, is taking you on . . ."—it seemed incredible to me, something that could only be a very cruel joke. But it was not. Not only because of the literary stimulus of his first novels, but also because of his generosity in the form of admiration and help, Carlos Fuentes has been one of the precipitating agents of the Boom. For better or for worse, his name goes on being linked with it as much for his reality as for the legend of his Mafia and his cohorts.

My correspondence with Carl Brandt, who later would become one of my best friends, began then, and the prospect of being published in the United States, not by one of the university presses or by one of these shady, fly-by-night concerns which at that time were publishing some authors "from south of the border" as curiosity pieces, but by the publisher of Thomas Mann, E. M. Forster, and Albert Camus, seemed to place within my reach all the possibilities corresponding, on another level, to those that the reading of *Where the Air Is Clear* had offered me.

4

ONE OF THE AXIOMS which feeds the envy of the "enemies" of the Boom is the fantasy that, thanks to their substantial author's rights, the Boom's principal members lead lazy lives of luxury in the most fascinating capitals of the world, traveling by jet from the Via Veneto to Madison Avenue and to St. Germain-des-Prés; and that the printings and successes of the translations of their books in the United States and on the other side of the Atlantic astonish the whole world.

Like all products of paranoia, this gilded vision of the success of Latin American writers—the absurd carnival which the legend has annexed to a much more serious but much less splendid reality—is, clearly, totally mistaken.

Outside of García Márquez with his fabulous *One Hundred Years of Solitude*, I do not believe that the author's rights of any Latin American writer can justifiably be called "substantial." On the contrary, the life of the Boom writers is and has been rather difficult and their greatest struggle is to steal a few hours for writing from the work that grants them a modest subsistence. The very same García Márquez, who barely survived by writing film scripts in Mexico, left work when *One Hundred Years of Solitude* had ripened inside him and he was ready to write, knowing that he and his family would experience poverty. Thanks to the money lent him by such friends as the Colombian poet Alvaro Mutis, he was able to go into seclusion to write the most talked-about novel in Spanish that I can remember. *One Hundred Years of Solitude* was published in 1967. From then on, certainly, the triumph at the level of commotion and scandal of García Márquez' novel—and I must clarify that the "scandal" is a product, above all, of how unbearable it is to some people that a book of such literary quality can also be an unprecedented public success—has made it the *only* novel whose sales may justifiably be called "substantial." And only as of 1969 could the Colombian novelist enjoy the "luxury" of living where and how he wants and of writing when he wants, besides taking pleasure in imposing his own conditions on the publishers and the movie producers who surround him. It therefore must be emphasized that only with *One Hundred Years of Solitude* can one talk about a "triumph" in a popular and commercial sense. Before *One Hundred Years of Solitude* and despite the proportionately greater successes of other writers of the Boom, the success had been, more than anything else, literary, confined to an elite, each time more extensive, certainly, but always an elite. In other words, the "commercialization" to which Miguel Angel Asturias alluded in his speech in Salamanca in 1971, and again in his declarations to a local newspaper that the writers of the Boom were "mere products of publicity," can be understood only in relation to García Márquez and only beginning with *One Hundred Years of Solitude;* because, before that book, the Spanish American novel, including the works which won the illustrious Nobel Prize, had never been great commercial successes, not even—as the Guatemalan understood perfectly—sufficient to maintain a modest independence.

It must be remembered, nevertheless, that this legend of luxury was born with Carlos Fuentes, who, in the first moment of the Boom, embodied for the devouring eyes of the writers of an entire continent that triumph, that fame, that power, even that cosmopolitan "luxury" which from the isolated Latin American capitals seemed impossible to obtain and which still is connected to the writers of the Boom. He was the first to handle his works through literary agents, the first to have friendships with the important writers of Europe and North America—James Jones loans him his apartment in a famous hotel on the Ile-St. Louis; Mandiargues and William Styron receive him as a friend—the first to be considered a novelist of the first rank by North American critics, the first to realize the magnitude of what was happening in the Spanish American novel of his generation, and, generously and chivalrously, the first to make it known. His flamboyant character colored and gave shape to the phenomenon itself as viewed by a growing public. But even for Fuentes, who, outside of having his own earnings which he supplements with work for publishing houses and movie studios, things have not been as easy as it appears, not even in that first moment of the Boom, when he embodied it and really could say: *"Le Boom c'est moi."* He has never had the fame, the true fame of a popular novelist beyond the range of the Spanish language, despite *Mademoiselle*'s telling its readers: *Hâtez-vous, mesdames, connaissez Fuentes.* When he arrived at the offices of Gallimard, his publisher in France, for the first time, to ask to meet the director who had just bought his first novel, the secretary asked him for his name and he told her. The secretary's look continued to be inquisitive and disconcerted as if she were waiting for clarification which Fuentes hastened to provide: *"Je suis un romancier mexicain. . . ."* In the presence of something so incredible, the secretary could not restrain a *"Sans blague . . . !"*

Among the novelists of the Boom, Carlos Fuentes is undoubtedly the person who moves around the most, who organizes the most congresses, who receives the most letters and invents the most projects—projects destined to radiate their light over a large number of the writers of his generation. More than any other, I remember one project which seemed sensational to me and which was going to be published simultaneously by I have no idea how many European and American publishing houses. It had to do with writing a book jointly on the great political figures of Latin America that would be called *Los Padres de las Patrias* (The Fathers of the Fatherlands). I remember that Vargas Llosa was to write about Odría, Jorge Edwards about Balmaceda, I about Melgarejo, Cortázar about Eva Perón (I understand that this part is written and consists of a fantasy in which Eva Perón's cadaver is rotting and infesting all of Buenos Aires), until the book would have a dozen writers, each responsible for one political figure. Much talked-about, this project was never carried out. Such things have given Fuentes the reputation of a literary manipulator and, consequently, those whom Fuentes does not support for personal or literary reasons do not miss an opportunity to slander his work. In regard to Fuentes, it is necessary to say that although his production is undoubtedly one of the most respected in Latin America and one of the best known and most studied in the United States and Europe, the author's royalties that the translations have yielded him are far from being as "substantial" as fantasy would have it; and as far as Spain is concerned, his name, for obvious reasons, is less known to the public which knows Cortázar, Vargas Llosa, and García Márquez only too well.

In regard to Julio Cortázar and his "enormous international prestige," as well as his soft life as a cosmopolitan writer based for over twenty years in Paris, there is much to be clarified. Just his twenty years in Paris would be enough to have rocks thrown at him by a whole aggressive phalanx of puritan writers, who still maintain that a writer must live in his own country and, if he does not, that he is a traitor. The public and critical failure of *Hopscotch* in France and Italy has been one of the great calamities for his Spanish-speaking admirers: too European, said the newspapers, too cosmopolitan, too intellectual, we do this sort of thing better ourselves, and it is absolutely not what is expected from a Spanish American novelist, neither like García Márquez, for example, nor even like Lezama Lima at his most difficult, whose *Paradiso* had an unexpected success in France. It is well known, on the other hand, that for years *Hopscotch* has been the object of an enthusi-

59

astic cult in universities in the United States; that is to say, in one of the few settings in that country capable of absorbing literature as literature. But the university population of the United States is immense, incalculable, and *Hopscotch*, therefore, has had an enormous circulation there. In certain sectors of Spain the matter is divided between the Cortazarians and the Lezamists, irreconcilable enemies despite the Argentine's stupendous admiration for the Cuban. I have heard more than one Lezamist intellectual state in regard to any novel he does not like: "Terrible. He writes almost as badly as Cortázar." Despite this, it is true that Cortázar's success in Spanish has been phenomenal. But that does not bring economic success. Cortázar works with UNESCO as a translator, he lives in an apartment in Paris, and as his only "luxury" has a very modest little house in Vaucluse, where he secludes himself to write when he can. In any case, his relative "international fame" is due more than anything else to the popular success of the movie *Blow-Up*, based on his short story "Las babas del diablo" (The Devil's Spittle). Cortázar says that when he was in Teheran for a UNESCO conference he entered a supermarket to buy toothpaste. As usual, he went up to the book racks. There he saw a pocketbook edition of *Hopscotch* in English, with the cover filled with rather naked women. In addition to the tiny name of the author and the title, the publishers had managed to wedge into all that feminine anatomy a blurb which said: Love, Sex, Passion, Sin, by the author of *Blow-Up*.

Mario Vargas Llosa embodies the second phase of the Boom: the great explosion was produced in 1962, when, still a twenty-four-year-old, he received the Biblioteca Breve Prize from the Barcelona publishing house of Seix

Barral. With that prize and a great deal of hoopla, his name—and, incidentally, that of Seix Barral Publishers—suddenly became popular in the entire Spanish-speaking world. *The Time of the Hero* caused the whole continent to talk. Perhaps it would not be too risky to offer the opinion that its success was in part due to the fame and "maneuverings" of Carlos Fuentes, who had fertilized the land so that the thing could take root. Vargas Llosa, like García Márquez, and like Fuentes at times, has lived in a cosmopolitan manner, at the start in France, where he wrote *The Time of the Hero* while working for RTF, later in England and until recently in Barcelona. But despite the thunderous success of *The Time of the Hero*, he had to continue working night after night for RTF in Paris. And later, when he moved to London with his wife and two small children, to teach at the University of London, Vargas Llosa lived in such severe and wretched circumstances that his home consisted of two furnished rooms— he would lock himself up in one while his wife tried to keep the children relatively quiet so that in the next room Vargas Llosa could finish *Conversation in The Cathedral*. Any time they had free from working and caring for the children was spent in hunting the rats which infested the apartment, and when they were not hunting them, they were talking about them: how many did you see yesterday, it looks like there's one under the table, I killed three, they ate the bed, etc. Nowadays, in more comfortable economic conditions, and able—at the moment, since Vargas Llosa is thinking about the possibility of returning to teaching—to devote all his time to writing, he stops at times in the middle of a conversation with his wife and after a short meditative silence he expresses his astonishment at their not talking about rats or hunting them as they did in London. The success of Vargas Llosa's novels in translation has been good, but very far from what his enemies fantasize. Einaudi, for example, left the original of *The Green House* in a box for an entire year before doing anything with it. Rowohlt, in Germany, has been unable to excite the public with the Peruvian's books. In the United States, despite mistaken criticism in some quarters, his books have made it to paperback editions. And in England *The Time of the Hero* obtained the rank of a classic when it was published by Penguin Books.

From my point of view, the third phase—and perhaps the definitive moment of the Latin American Boom as a Boom—occurs with the publication of *One Hundred Years of Solitude* by Gabriel García Márquez. In the case of this author one can truly speak of an infinity of "substantial" things: his success in Spanish has been such that the author has come to be part of the mythology, resounding in every country, in nearly every translation, or, at least, certainly in all the ones I know, and still more certainly in comparison to the critical and public successes of all the other authors who write in Spanish. One edition untiringly follows another: one speaks in terms of millions of copies. In the United States the novel figured among the best sellers, and despite the huge sales, despite the immense prestige which his name has acquired in the United States, despite the respect given the republication of his earlier books, the critic for *Time* magazine still referred to *One Hundred Years of Solitude* as a book about which "everyone talks but not everyone reads." And this is explicable: fantastic as the number of its editions are for a Latin American writer, in the United States they cannot be compared to those of a Leon Uris or a Mario Puzo about whom everyone really does talk and whom everyone really does read. Gabriel García Márquez is now able to live in Barcelona in a "luxury" that would seem very modest in comparison to the luxury of popular authors and publishers, of those with palaces and yachts. One of García Márquez' best-known lines is "All publishers are rich and all writers are poor. . . ." Perhaps the most curious fact by which to measure the extent of his popularity was something I encountered when I was reading the Italian translation of a pornographic Russian novel. In one episode, the male protagonist who represents the new, corrupt, and westernized Russia, a boy who does not deny himself any pleasure, reclines on the seat of his Volga automobile while he awaits the woman with whom he has an amorous date, turns on the radio and opens the magazine *Foreign Literature* to read—as is obviously being read everywhere—another installment of *One Hundred Years of Solitude*.

The lists of the hardships and sacrifices of the Latin American novelists could be continued *ad infinitum* in order to disprove the fascinating legend that they are fed exclusively on a diet which consists of "martinis toasting the health of the Fellinis", in order to refute the vaunted international reputations which those who were left behind refer to but which, unfortunately, are in reality only relative. For example, Onetti, one of the great novelists of the continent, remains infuriatingly unknown; Borges—subsidized by a wealthy and intelligent father until he was thirty-six and then employed as a librarian and a professor—had to become famous abroad before he was transformed into a national monument; Martínez Moreno works obscurely in his law office in Montevideo; Sábato, a prisoner of self-destructive ghosts that have delayed the appearance of *Sobre héroes y tumbas* (About Heroes and Tombs) in English for over a decade even though that book had a greater success than *Hopscotch* in Italy, is shackled, timid, unable to put himself in a position where his work will obtain the renown it unquestionably deserves and which everyone offers; Garmendia, David Viñas, Beatriz Guido, Alejo Carpentier, all the novelists who are more or less connected to the amorphous Boom, are hardly famous among the elite or specialists abroad, and have to depend on other earnings or activities in order to survive, in the majority of cases, rather modestly. Only Juan Rulfo's fame—to say about him what T. S. Eliot said about E. M. Forster—grows with each book that he does not write.

By all of this I want to illustrate the legend circulating in certain parts of Latin America about the fabulous success of the Boom novelists in the United States and in Europe—the idea that "they are fashionable." That is nothing more than a relative truth. That they are spoken of more than before, that prestigious publishers fight to obtain their books, that critics receive them with an admiration not without surprise, that the translations multiply and spread, that universities organize departments to study Latin American literature impelled more than anything else by the culmination of the contemporary novel—all of this is certain. But from this to "being fashionable," from this to being writers like Golding or Lawrence Durrell fifteen years ago, the distance is huge. It must be made clear that in the majority of countries the translations of our novels are always reviewed in the press by professors of Latin American literature, and they appear in the important newspapers not next to the novels from the rest of the world but beneath some heading or within a frame—*Amérique Latine, Romanciers Latinoaméricains*—which is a form of exclusion. It must also be noted that for better or for worse the publicity for the Latin American novel is in the hands of officious agents of the publishing houses or often depends on personal friendships, on good or bad relations with professors, writers, critics, and influential people. And there are some countries, like Germany for example, which are totally recalcitrant toward the Latin American novel, totally refusing to give it any importance and where the few books published by Rowohlt or by the smaller publishing houses have not received acceptance nor caused the smallest repercussion in any class in Germany. The majority of the books printed lie covered with dust in cellars in Hamburg and Frankfurt.

Why, then, and how do such a large number of Latin American novelists live in self-exile? Exile is another of the legendary elements which the Latin American critics seldom pardon, and by condemning the writers for "living away from national problems," they are accusing them of a rootless cosmopolitanism. But the accusations which this voluntary exile—another of the characteristics that, freely applied, would give shape to the hypothetical Boom—brings upon itself are no more than a variation of the accusation directed in all periods at the Latin American writers who almost always have lived for long periods, at least, outside their countries: Darío and the modernists in Paris, where they founded the magazine *Mundial*, so similar to other of today's magazines based in Paris; Neruda, Borges, Vallejo in Paris and in Spain, all of them, at one time in their lives, were voluntary exiles. It must be remembered that in the first half of this century poetry enjoyed the prestige which the novel enjoys today, but poetry came to be too elitist a form—something which could well happen to the novel if it follows some of the directions being indicated for it and if we believe McLuhan—and the novel took its place: novelists, then, became invested with the aura that a half century earlier had invested poetry.

One of the characteristics of Latin American poets in the first half of this century was the way in which they cultivated literary friendships, something which was easily done because they all came from different countries and therefore the acquaintances were not harmful. Such "friendships"—sometimes called a "Mafia" by those who feel themselves excluded—are often thrown into the faces of the present-day novelists who are accused of blowing each other's horns, of writing about each other, of maintaining a type of united front of admiration tolerating neither criticism nor examination. Besides the fact that the friendships among today's Latin American novelists are rather relative—and in some cases nonexistent, sometimes reaching frank hostility—there remains the fact that the phenomenon of the Latin American novel of the '60s is of such interest to the world that very few of those who are related to it in any way can or want to stop examining or writing about it. Beyond this there are precedents in modernist poetry, for example, when Santos Chocano wrote a letter to Darío in which he wildly speculates at his having sent Darío a copy of his latest book several months ago, asking him how it is possible that he still has not written anything about it, urging him to do so soon. Was this also blowing each other's horns?

One of the things least understood in Europe—in Spain, in Italy—is this friendship or at least the generally good relation among Latin American novelists today. Perhaps they do not realize that one of the most important elements is that the continent is made up of twenty-one different republics and even if literary friendships within one country are usually difficult, they are not difficult in an international sphere. For example, it would be very strange for the Colombians to accept with equanimity the fact that Gabriel García Márquez' name may almost completely obscure, independently of his own will, all the other names of contemporary Colombian narrative. To hear many Mexican writers speak of "that boy Fuentes"— "boy" in that he unpardonably belongs to the upper bourgeoisie—and to hear how they question his skills and his achievements is to have one of the cruelest experiences of the destructiveness of envy within the literary life of a country. In Buenos Aires Cortázar is followed down the street in admiration, but they speak badly of him, they create imaginary fights which end in quarrels and enmities, as for example between Sábato and him. In Peru, where the literary stature of Vargas Llosa has also thrown a shadow over the other writers of that country, ambivalence, admiration, and hatred have gone from the extreme of announcing during a movie in a cinema in Lima that the movie house in question has the great honor of greeting the illustrious writer Mario Vargas Llosa who is seated in the audience, to the other extreme of the most merciless political and literary attacks.

But when national boundaries are crossed and the novel becomes international, good relations are possible. Not only good relations but often the valuable admiration of one writer for another's work. An Italian critic passing through Barcelona was once at a get-together attended by both Vargas Llosa and another Latin American novelist. When he saw them laughing together and talking during a cocktail party, he said: "In Italy, it would be impossible for a writer like Vargas Llosa to write a book about the work of another writer like García Márquez. And for both of them to be at the same party without one throwing poison into the other's coffee, well, that really would seem like science fiction."

This critic did not consider that when we leave our chauvinistic and competitive provinces, generally the literary sect formed within each country, envy becomes minimal. Is this not, perhaps, one of the reasons for the fact that most of the major novels of the Boom were written outside their respective countries, and that so many Latin American novelists continuing to leave their own countries in order to become neighbors abroad? Obviously, we cannot talk of a mere coincidence if Cortázar, García Márquez, Vargas Llosa, Cabrera Infante, Severo Sarduy, Salvador Garmendia, Jorge Edwards, Augusto Monterroso, Carpentier, Carlos Fuentes, and Mario Benedetti are living or have lived for so long outside their countries. The motives for exile may be numerous and varied, from easily formulated political reasons to the most ambiguous causes that might force them to flee the ghosts suffocating and drowning them in their own countries. In any case, it cannot be denied that exile, cosmopolitanism, internationalization, all more or less connected, have shaped a very considerable part of the Latin American narrative of the 1960s.

5

IT IS OFTEN said that the "popularity" of the contemporary Spanish American novel is in large part due to the efficiency of the publicity mechanism that publishing houses have set in motion in order to launch the books they are determined to sell. This legend has spread, confirmed by the authority of Miguel Angel Asturias, who declared that "some" of today's Spanish American novelists are "mere products of publicity." But the cruel truth is that not even the enormous publicity which the Nobel Prize signifies has obtained for the Guatemalan what the modest launching by Sudamericana obtained for *One Hundred Years of Solitude*.

In any case, the phenomenon of publicity is not disgraceful: it is something very much of our times, and the duty of a contemporary writer who has the power is, precisely, to demand this publicity from his publishers, to demand that they do a great deal to push a book, because if the novelist does not make this demand publicity will be sacrificed to company profits. The demand for publicity is one of the most justifiable forms that the writer's fight against the concerns of the company—commercial or state-owned—can take, and it is the author's undeniable right in societies more developed than ours. Besides being a snobbery totally without distinction in our time, the gesture of the romantic writer who dies undiscovered in his garret in order not to dirty himself with anything so sordid as publicity turns out to be an impossibility: greedy for original works, there are too many publishers keeping their commercial and printing machinery in constant motion for the writer with any talent at all to die unrecognized.

The most effective publicity which in the '60s has accelerated the pulse of the Spanish American novel and has made it, if not as popular as legend would have it, certainly very widely known, is unquestionably the appearance within a very short time of a number of novels that have captured the public imagination. In the space of two years (1962–1964) I read *Hopscotch*, *Sobre héroes y tumbas* (About Heroes and Tombs), *The Time of the Hero*, *The Death of Artemio Cruz*, *Pedro Páramo* and *The Burning Plain*, *The Winners* and the short stories of Cortázar, *The Shipyard* by Onetti; and just a little earlier I had read *The Lost Steps*, *Where the Air Is Clear*, and all that Borges had published up until then. After my departure from Chile for Mexico in 1965, the first thing I did abroad was to read *No One Writes to the Colonel* by Gabriel García Márquez. No publicity apparatus, not even the most perfect, would have been able to produce these coincidences; and it is only because of poor publicity and distribution that, in spite of *The Time of the Hero*'s having received a prize in 1962, I obtained the book only at the end of 1964.

After the early '60s, it was impossible for the public interested in the novel as literature—in contrast to the public that only reads to be "entertained" or to those who read because they are interested in the things literature points to beyond itself, but not in literary complexity as such—to be unaware that something new was happening in the Spanish American novel. But in 1962, even the public that only follows the fads began to take notice of the legitimate publicity surrounding Mario Vargas Llosa's *The Time of the Hero* which that year won the Biblioteca Breve Prize for the Novel from Editorial Seix Barral—one of the few literary prizes that has stayed literarily solvent for such a long time and, despite its not being endowed with a great amount of money, has wisely stimulated the dissemination of present trends in the novel. Starting with *The Time of the Hero*, the public began to ask: Who is Mario Vargas Llosa? What is the contemporary Spanish American novel? What is the Biblioteca Breve? What is Seix Barral? It was obvious that a Spanish publishing house that gave so much importance to the first novel of a twenty-four-year-old Peruvian writer had to be a company with a new attitude, a company prepared to align itself with the new writers and to be their means of communication. And just as the Biblioteca Breve Prize for the Novel in 1962 "launched" Mario Vargas Llosa, it is equally justifiable to say that Mario Vargas Llosa "launched" Seix Barral. The year before, in Yugoslavia, Miodrag Bulatovic asked me if he had

71

done the right thing in giving the Spanish rights to *Un gallo rojo vuela hasta el cielo* (A Red Rooster Flies Up to Heaven) to Seix Barral, and I answered that I did not know, that Seix Barral seemed to me to be a publishing house without any great distinction. But after *The Time of the Hero*, Seix Barral began to acquire a character very much its own, and the success of the Latin American novel of the '60s is joined to this publishing house and to the name of Carlos Barral.

As usual, the problem in Chile was one of literary isolation: the difficulty of obtaining books. Alastair Reid passed through Santiago, and one night in my home in the Los Dominicos section of the city he spoke to me for the first time of Mario Vargas Llosa and his extraordinary talent. He assured me that *The Time of the Hero* was a great novel and that the author was an exceptional person although still very young; he said that if Vargas Llosa could rid himself of certain limitations—his acquaintance and nearly exclusive engagement with the world of the masculine "clique"—he would become one of the great novelists of his time. From Barcelona Alastair Reid had a copy of *The Time of the Hero* sent to me (he passed through Chile in 1963; I received the novel in 1964, two years after the prize), and in reading it I realized that literary prizes could be more than a commercial gambit, that they could have, finally, a function and a purpose: that of initiating a literary career and that of aligning it with a new movement. The prize also meant that in Europe and in Spain, Latin Americans did not belong to a race inferior to that of the demigods we were reading then: Cela, Ana María Matute, García Hortelano, Sánchez Ferlosio, Miguel Delibes, Juan Goytisolo. I wrote a review of *The Time of the Hero* for the newspaper *Ercilla* where I was then working, but readers of my literary page could not find the book anywhere because it took another year to arrive in the bookstores. On the other hand, books from Spanish publishers have something suspiciously *vieullot* in their presentation even though their quality may be as solid as that of *El Jarama* (The Jarama) by Sánchez Ferlosio or as immediately seductive as that of *Primera memoria* (First Memory) by Ana María Matute. But the Biblioteca Breve of Seix Barral, with its audacious, brilliant, and up-to-date photograph on the cover was the envy of all of us who had to put up with the total lack of style and the defective presentation of most Latin American books.

In Mexico there was the wonderful publishing house of Fondo de Cultura Económica; but, after Orfila's departure, it specialized almost exclusively in philosophical and cultural subjects, leaving the literary aside; meantime, little by little, Joaquín Mortiz was organizing a publishing house with an appearance not very different from Seix Barral's. In Buenos Aires there were the powerful and prestigious houses that nourished us during the lean years of the wars: Losada, Emecé, Sudamericana, SUR. But these publishers were either totally turned toward Europe and the United States, publishing the most important things they could find abroad, or publishing work after work from the arrogant and closed Olympus of the River Plate. These publishing houses never—or seldom, so as not to fall into restrictive statements without a statistical base—published or considered for publication contemporary novelists from other Latin American countries. Angel Rama is correct in stating that ". . . the lack of internal communication in Latin America is what explains that the

73

different regions are connected and known through foreign centers. . . ." The connection was effected, more often than not, through Barcelona and, specifically, through Seix Barral. For years Sudamericana had been publishing the excellent short stories of Julio Cortázar in a sepulchral silence. Can it then be said that Cortázar is a product of publicity if his short stories, now international classics, lay buried for years in a small *coterie* of the River Plate where Ana María Barrenechea acted as High Priestess? In 1959 Emecé gave a first prize to *El huésped* (The Guest), a novel by the Chilean Margarita Aguirre—a life-long friend with whom I had roller-skated on the streets of the Providencia section of that Santiago of streetcars and adolescence—but, now that she was married to a well-to-do Argentine, she was no longer a foreigner in Buenos Aires. The other countries had almost no publishing houses. I remember the dreadful Peruvian editions of Sebastián Salazar Bondy and José María Arguedas that I obtained, not because they were sold in Chile but because Salazar Bondy was in the habit of traveling to Santiago and carrying books as in a courier service of Indian *chasquis* [1] that at that time—and up until the second half of the '6os—was the only way to circulate what was being written. For a while in Chile the monopoly practically maintained a blockade against the importation and distribution of books because the lower cost and superior quality of imported books competed with what they produced. Besides, it was impossible for foreign publishers to take the profits from the sales of their books out of Chile. As a result the country suffered a prolonged literary asphyxiation.

But fortunately I had traveled and I continued to travel.

[1] *Chasqui* is the Incan word for messenger or courier. [G.K.]

74

And Salazar Bondy traveled and Ernesto Sábato traveled and Angel Rama traveled and Carlos Fuentes traveled, and we carried and brought back books in our lightened luggage in order to give them to our friends, to people who read, to people who wrote and reviewed, to people who were interested in the new things being written in our world. And we traveled again with our suitcases packed with books, like literary *chasquis*, in order to have a drink with friends and to talk about books in other capitals of the continent. Passing through Montevideo on a trip to Europe in the 1950s I established contact with several Uruguayan writers to whom I sent my books as they appeared. The first foreign notices of my works appeared in Montevideo; but from there to the point where the Uruguayan public would have my books within reach was another matter. I remember how I loaned *Hopscotch* and *Sobre héroes y tumbas* (About Heroes and Tombs) to the Chilean novelist Juan Agustín Palazuelos—who joined Sábato against Cortázar, since he compulsively had to enlist in favor of someone and against someone else—later passing them from hand to hand until I lost what must have been one of the few copies of *Sobre héroes y tumbas* circulating in Chile. As late as 1966 it was impossible to obtain *Hopscotch* in Santiago: I have a letter from Mercedes Valdivieso—I was in the United States and she was in Chile—begging me to tell her how she could get *Hopscotch*, about which so much was being said but which seemed to have a ghostly existence because it could not be found in the bookstores. In 1964, Sonia Vidal, after a triumphant singing tour of the night clubs of Mexico, brought me as a gift the books of Juan Rulfo, a writer then little known among us. No one was worried about relieving this poverty: the idea persisted in the minds of the distributors that the Spanish American novel continued to stagnate in the same situation as before, in the period of *costumbrista* and *criollista* isolation, and that it was incapable of being of international interest. Nothing came in, nothing went out: the only effective thing was that courier service of *chasquis* which, I suppose, must have been what gave birth to the legend that Spanish American writers are joined in a Mafia of mutual propaganda.

But something else was hatching. The storm would begin to break loose in 1962: it was without a doubt the amazement of the public and of the young writers at the literary prize given in Spain to a Peruvian novel, written by an author of so much talent and so few years as Mario Vargas Llosa, which initially contributed to letting loose the uproar, the famous Boom that would be heard everywhere. I remember how my wife asked Juan Agustín Palazuelos, then twenty-four, in order to anger him:

"Do you know how old Vargas Llosa was when he wrote *The Time of the Hero?*"

"No."

"As old as you."

And Palazuelos, who never went for long without his repartee, immediately responded:

"And do you know how old Camus was when they gave him the Nobel Prize?"

"No. . ."

"The same age as your husband."

I had written a letter to Elsa Arana of the newspaper *Siete días* in Lima, expressing my admiration for *The Time of the Hero* but also speaking of my discouragement, of my sense of a lack of stimulation, of the certainty of the total

76

impossibility of realizing an especially significant work if I remained confined in Chile. The discouragement I expressed in that letter was due—in addition to an enormous and justifiable envy mixed with admiration for the author of *The Time of the Hero*—to a feeling, certainly very subjective, very personal, that for me it was already too late, that I was paralyzed, writing and rewriting version after version, year after year, of *The Obscene Bird of Night* which was swelling but not growing. I was approaching forty years of age and I was the author of only two little books of short stories and of *Coronation*, while that inexperienced kid. . . .

The stimulus I received from reading *The Time of the Hero* was due in part to the envy its quality produced in me, in part to the uproar that occurred as its fame began to spread. On the purely literary level, Vargas Llosa was assuredly concerned with the problem of point of view— around which are developed the narrative techniques of writers from Joseph Conrad and Henry James onward, writers who, manipulating the point of view, each in his own manner, substitute for the old narrative thread of the first person or of the omniscient narrator complicated formal structures which constitute true experiments in the possibilities of the novel. In *The Time of the Hero* the Peruvian played strange and perturbing games with point of view: he experimented consciously and intellectually; meanwhile, he placed himself in a position of investigating the very nature of the novel, advancing further and further—until reaching a zenith in *Conversation in The Cathedral*—toward the elimination of the narrating and expressive intermediary in order to arrive at a totally objectified art. How was it possible, then, that the Latin American public did not find this experimentation, which I would never have dared to undertake, "pretentious"? Carlos Fuentes had already worried about point of view in *Where the Air Is Clear* but the question beyond the technique of experimenting with point of view—which presumes a criticism by the novelist of his own work—was buried too deeply in the excessively sumptuous fleshiness of that novel. *The Time of the Hero*, on the other hand, with its manipulation of point of view as a technical support, tackles the question head on and without hesitation. Experimentation. Technical problems. Estheticism, despite the naturalism which occupies the forefront of the story. Literature of an elite, taboo: therefore, in our circumstances, intellectual, pretentious, and decadent, what really mattered was what was simple, the directly pertinent, the topical, the journalistic. At the very most, a "magical realism" might be accepted. *The Time of the Hero* has absolutely nothing to do with magic. It is a novel whose execution and intention are predominately intellectual. Nevertheless, despite demolishing so many taboos—or perhaps because it did—*The Time of the Hero* has had and continues to have an enormous success after more than ten years; and its success is supported not only by the common reader, who continues to buy it, but also by literary necessity.

Whom to write for, then? On a personal level I proposed for myself the undermining of rules and with their collapse, the opening of new possibilities. How to write, to whom to address myself? Was Pablo Neruda right when on one occasion he told my wife that I should write "the great social novel of Chile" since no one felt "the chill of poverty" as I did? Or were Fuentes, Cortázar, Sábato, and Vargas Llosa right, in pointing not to the path of directness—and in that sense Neruda's statement is the definitive accolade—but rather to the dangerous path of experimentation, with the risk of solitude, of not being understood, of not having a ruler with which to measure the value of what was invented? That is to say: the admirable, voluntary obscurity which those writers placed between themselves and their readers, between themselves and the common reader in Latin America, was a challenge to bourgeois complacency to transcend the anecdotal, the topical.

These books, suddenly dispersed by the travels of the *chasquis*, produced a consciousness among the novelists that they could write for a more literarily mature public, that the common reader in Latin America was now more sophisticated. It was the appearance of this mature, continental, and international public that so radically changed our world in the mid '60s. Now the audience proposed to the novelist was not limited to that writer's own country but, instead, was the entire Spanish-speaking world. It was now clear that this public was interested in literature as such and not merely as an extension of pedagogy, patriotism, or history. This became evident with the sudden popularity of Borges as a result, naturally, of his discovery in the United States, Italy, and France, and with the Biblioteca Breve Prize going to a twenty-four-year-old Peruvian writer, the author of a novel which at that time could well be qualified as "difficult." In the cafes and in social gatherings and in the parks, Cortázar and Sábato were spoken about more than the others because this new literature of experimentation, this new, "difficult" literature, was the forceful means for beating back either the *cos-*

tumbrista romanticism or that romanticism weighed down by a heavy social pretext in the immediately preceding novels. This new literature was to abolish forever the cliché that to the "essential," which had to be ours, was opposed the "intellectual," which had to be foreign, esthetic, taboo. Why should *Finnegans Wake* or *Nightwood* be understood only in Europe? Was it not a form of self-respect to write as one felt, to write something as proportionately difficult as *Finnegans Wake* or *Nightwood*, even though it might be totally different from those works?

Sábato was also brought to Chile by the *chasquis*. I met him one afternoon in one of those celebrated meetings in Santiago at Lolito Echeverría's home, where for over forty years a literary gathering met daily around that ancient aristocrat—very Chilean, elegant, ignorant, who officiated, nearly every day of his life, for the friends of her admired Hernán Díaz Arrieta. I remained in the background, listening in silence to Sábato, without his remembering that we had met years before at Pedro Echagüe's home in Buenos Aires. I listened to the uninterrupted flow of the multicolored streamers of his ideas tinted with River Plate metaphysics and *Angst;* I saw him as an omnivore, uncertain, histrionic, intelligent, arrogant, curious, sensitive, tremendously vulnerable. His untiring eyes scrutinized everything while he fulfilled his role of *vedette* at that gathering: they examined the immense romantic painting of flowers which covered nearly an entire wall of the salon; the servants who circulated with whiskey, tea, scented water, and *petits fours;* he looked straight at the dean of Chilean criticism, installed in his pontifical seat of honor from which he refuted Sábato with that Chilean tranquility of men like José Santos González

Vera, Enrique Espinoza, Armando Uribe, of a Santiago that seemed impossible to disturb. Sábato's stenographic eyes were noting all of it: his Argentine antennae were taking it all in. Immediately, I read *Sobre héroes y tumbas* (About Heroes and Tombs), given to me by Sábato's personal *chasqui* in Chile, Edmundo Concha. This uneven and marvelous book fell into my hands just when I was obsessively writing and rewriting *The Obscene Bird of Night* in the hope of finding a rational form for it. Just as reading *The Time of the Hero* had freed me from the shackles binding me to a static point of view in the novel, *Sobre héroes y tumbas* also seemed to me to be a novel aimed directly against my taboos, more than anything because it made me realize that to attempt to give a rational form to something that I myself was living as an obsession was not only a behavioral mistake but also a literary one. Sábato's novel made me realize that the irrational could have intellectual significance equal to or even greater than the rational, and that at times it can disguise itself as rationality; that "intelligence" and "irrationality" are not contradictory words; that the irrational and the obsessive can have great literary standing, as Sábato gave them in *Sobre héroes y tumbas*, and that the ghosts of the irrational hide in things that pursue us daily with their concealed presences. I realized that, unrestrained and chaotic, the rational and the intellectual can proliferate like a cancer and give to a novel such as *Sobre héroes y tumbas* this unhealthy, cancerous air.

Carrying it as a gift from Buenos Aires, my wife was the *chasqui* who introduced me to *The Winners*, as well as to all the short stories that Julio Cortázar had published by that time. She had been an admirer of his ever since she attended Ana María Barrenechea's lectures at the Faculty of Philosophy and Letters in Buenos Aires. I read the stories with interest but without enthusiasm. I stayed outside of those tightly closed structures, which, nevertheless, under a bundle of vanguardist tinsel—as so often happens in Cortázar's work—conceal a classical architecture and a Cartesian mind that apparently obliges him to take up ludic poses that do not match his material and that are a sort of expiation. After all, his stories—like those of O. Henry, for example—frequently depend on the surprise ending, on the plot itself, and his attempt to hide this fact produces, at times, the spectacular corpulence of his writings. *The Winners*, on the other hand, seemed to me another version of *The Canterbury Tales,* of the *Decameron,* of *The Heptameron* of the Princess of Angulema made over in an Argentine style: a catalog of the social classes of Buenos Aires, of their types with their slang and customs and ethics—all coldly organized. There would be nothing wrong in all of this if he had not made the rationality of this classical architecture conflict with so much implicit material *à la manière de* Kafka without, however, reaching a synthesis: the collision leaves only a sort of floating Grand Hotel written by a Vicky Baum of great intellectual standing and of immense poetic invention. It must be remembered that if I judge Cortázar—like the others I may judge in these notes, since I have chosen my favorites from among all the Latin Americans in a totally subjective way without either pretending to be right or wanting to prove anything—I am doing it on a high level of exigency. A level of exigency that was totally satisfied when I read *Hopscotch.* Here the synthesis that did not occur in *The Winners* advances on a well-planted narrative mechanism displaying a self that is spectacularly persuasive, protean, intelligent, full of inventiveness, whose "cool" occupies its rightful place, who does not deform anything with his showy postures. Besides, Cortázar was a pure intellectual in continually ironizing about intellectuals, perhaps a form of modesty or an act of contrition before his inability to be a "common man"; but this continual act of contrition which is, on a certain level, *Hopscotch*, humanizes the novel and gives it feeling. Cortázar is a writer with the daring to treat intellectual snobbism, a writer with sufficient sophistication to see it, on the one hand, as a producer of guffaws and, on the other, to give it status inasmuch as he sees it embodying the anguished and powerless necessity of knowledge in a position out of step with society. He is an Argentine more Argentine than anyone else, precisely because he is engaged in so many things that are not Argentine; he is a novelist who dares to be discursive and whose pages are sprinkled with names of musicians, painters, art galleries, philosophers, movie directors—contemporary "culture" as such, all the sources which one had more or less approached while always attempting to hide it—all this had an undisguised place within his novel, something which I would never have dared to presume to be right for the Latin American novel, since it was fine for Thomas Mann but not for us. There is a story that one afternoon someone among a group of friends around a table in a Buenos Aires cafe asked Borges if he knew Sanskrit. Borges must have answered: "Well, I don't know; just the Sanskrit that everyone knows. . . ." *Hopscotch* raises that "Sanskrit that everyone knows" to its highest power, which is the language of the cultured bourgeoisie of the River Plate and in which Argentine novels are so often written. Therefore, contrary to what its detractors say in attacking it as an uprooted European work, *Hopscotch* rescues and appraises both a world and a language and from that point of view it must be seen as pure folklore.

Hopscotch, like the other novels of which I have spoken here, overthrew a great many of the literary dogmas that in my time I had seen as unquestionable. Even if I knew in a theoretical way that they were ruined—since I had read sufficiently to realize what was going on in other parts of the world—I still knew it only theoretically, the knowledge touched only my intelligence, suggesting another set of rules that merely contradicted the earlier ones. James, Proust, Faulkner, Joyce, Virginia Woolf, Mann, Céline . . . yes, very well, there they were, far away. The reading of Spanish American novels, on the other hand, not only got under my skin and entered my bloodstream but also, I think, permitted me, when I opened I have no idea which sluices, to incorporate the European and North American masters as something of my own.

I must make something clear: I never read the novels of which I am speaking here because I saw them advertised in magazines or because critics called my attention to them. I repeat: in essence, the detractors of the Boom who contend that everything is a question of friendships, cliques, mutual praise, are partly right. Who were going to make the books of the new novelists known at the beginning of the 1960s if not the friendly *chasquis* who traveled, sent and gave books, wrote letters, notes, criticism? Because of my astonishment at *Hopscotch* I wrote to my North American publishers so that they would buy the book without delay. They read it. They did not dare go along with it nor with *The Winners*, and they rejected them both: in the first half of the '60s, the United States was not prepared to absorb *Hopscotch* if it came from Latin

84

America. They could easily absorb Jorge Amado, for example, or *Coronation*. It is curious that in 1960 this novel would seem difficult. I have a letter from Harriet de Onís of that year, rejecting *Coronation* because it is not clear "on whose side the author is; whom he admires and whom he condemns. The same could be said of Faulkner, but Faulkner is great in spite of this, not because of it." The position of most Latin American novelists half a decade later, with their rejection of the Manichean vision of the world which the social novel had been advancing, would be exactly opposed to that of Harriet de Onís, who at that time controlled the sluices of the circulation of Latin American literature in the United States and, by means of the United States, throughout the whole world.

Until 1964 very few writers of my generation were translated in any comprehensive manner. The editions usually came from smaller publishing houses or from university presses. Very few writers had literary agents. What were literary agents, what purpose did they serve? We found ourselves obliged to journey from one publisher to the next with our manuscripts under our arms, begging them to publish our books. A commercial publicity stunt was exactly what we needed, up until a short while ago, to spare us from humiliation and hardship.

It is curious. In writing this I realize that not one, absolutely not one of the books of which I have spoken in this chapter, did I buy in a bookstore or because I was urged by reviews or criticism. All of them were given, stolen, carried, recommended by friends, sent in packages, or carried in the *chasquis'* suitcases. Alicia Jurado and Pipino Moreno-Hueyo, in Buenos Aires, gave me Borges' books. Juan Orrego Salas brought me *The Lost Steps* from Caracas. Montserrat Sanz gave me *Where the Air Is Clear*. Sonia

Vidal brought me *The Burning Plain* and *Pedro Páramo* from Mexico. Alastair Reid had the publisher send me a copy of *The Time of the Hero*. Edmundo Concha sent me *Sobre héroes y tumbas*. Carlos Fuentes himself sent me *The Death of Artemio Cruz* from Mexico. And my wife brought me Cortázar from Buenos Aires.

I do not know if all the writers of my generation are prepared to agree with me in what I say or if their isolation was identical to mine. I do not know if Vicente Leñero or Guillermo Cabrera Infante can say that something similar to this happened in their own countries. I do not know if they would name the same novels I have named among the contemporary Latin American novels which have had such a defining role. I am inclined to think that in many cases they would name other novels, since the constitution of the Boom is very elastic, not to say vague. But I suspect that, leaving out differences of personality and nationality, their experiences cannot have been too different from mine. What the detractors of the Boom declare is the pure truth: the writers themselves were responsible for a large part of the modest publicity that was created in a period that now seems so distant and so different because no one worried then about sending or discussing the books if the writers did not do it themselves. On their own, the Spanish American novelists, who today have reached maturity and who were then relatively young, undertook that curious enterprise opposed to the publishing and critical underdevelopment of our world, an enterprise which left behind the rubble of venerated esthetic dogmas, old prostheses now unused because of their excessive use in the past and corsets that had by now lost their ability to constrain.

6

I MUST REPEAT that I am not a professional critic; nor
a student who knows how to sprinkle his text with quotations in italics and with impressive footnotes from erudite
sources; nor a theoretician, master of a monolithic system
pretending to explain literary phenomena: everything that
I say is tentative, anecdotal, personal testimony, impression, approximation, and, therefore, refutable by other ev-
idence, other impressions, and other anecdotes. What I really am is a novelist. And, even more than that, a reader of
novels. I must confess this curious limitation to my intelligence: to read anything that is not a novel or that does
not refer to or have some relation to novels to me seems
lacking in substance—pale, schematic, a waste of time. I

87

understand the past—of course I understand it—illuminated more than anything by the novels I have read. And what can be understood of the present: gathered much more from the allusive world of novels than in the exhaustion of what is scientific or informative. Nevertheless, I do not read to learn. I read for another reason: for pleasure, but not to "entertain myself," which is something else. I prefer a thousand times to bore myself reading the masterful novels of Juan Benet because that gives me more pleasure than to "entertain myself" by reading Agatha Christie, who gives me nothing. With the years I have become one of those professionals who is only happy "talking shop," talking about my profession even in its smallest details. It is useless to search in these notes for anything more solid than the testimony I can give about the feelings and impressions awakened in me by certain novels and by the art of certain novelists, or the ideas I have put into practice relating them to each other and to the world which surrounds me and its fluctuations, to the events of my life and to the lives of other writers I have known.

The novelists I have known are for the most part the Spanish American novelists of my own and other generations, whether or not they belong to the Boom, which may or may not exist. And theirs are the novels, among the hundreds I have read in the last few years, that have most affected me: neither the writing of Purdy nor of Barth, neither that of Iris Murdoch nor of the *Tel Quel* circle, neither that of Günther Grass and Max Frisch nor of the recent Italians, neither that of Baldwin nor even of Styron and Vonnegut and the North American black humorists have seemed as pertinent or as close to me. As

Carlos Fuentes says in *Where the Air Is Clear:* "We fell here. What are we going to do? Endure, struggle." And the Spanish American writers have seemed pertinent to me, not because they clarify for once and for all what the essence of Buenos Aires is or what Lima was like in the time of Odría—things that do not much matter to me—but because, in spite of the differences in quality and orientation, I perceive a cohesiveness of origin and development, beginning with the breaking out of the national parish in the early '60s up to the courier service of the *chasquis*, which succeeded in forming a continental parish.

Because it was still a question of parochialism. The Latin American novel did not truly come into the world until the second half of the decade, starting with the scandalously unprecedented triumph of *One Hundred Years of Solitude* by Gabriel García Márquez, a Colombian with a reputation so skimpy that his name barely figured in the Congress of Intellectuals in Concepción in 1962, despite his having already published *No One Writes to the Colonel*. It has to be asserted that the Boom—noisy and vulgar and tarnished with the flattery and envy by which it is known today—gave a reason for publishers to pull hair from their beards in frustration for having rejected such-and-such a manuscript in which they did not know how to recognize quality; and it gave a reason, too, for the novelists—but only a few—to be able at last to impose modest conditions by means of literary agents, who soon began to collect Latin Americans. All of this begins only with *One Hundred Years of Solitude*.

It is true that in the decade of the 1960s five Biblioteca Breve Prizes for the Novel went to Latin Americans: *The Time of the Hero* by Mario Vargas Llosa, *Los albañiles* (The

Bricklayers) by Vicente Leñero, *Three Trapped Tigers* by Guillermo Cabrera Infante, *País portátil* (Portable Country) by Adriano González León, and *A Change of Skin* by Carlos Fuentes. Since the Biblioteca Breve Prize was in these years the only prize with authentic literary prestige in the Spanish-speaking world, the public lent its ears. And along with the listening, there arose an enemy courier service of *chasquis* who decisively influenced the Boom at its zenith: certain speakers traveled throughout the continent accusing the new novelists of living in exile, far from the problems of their countries, in a luxurious, sybaritic limbo abroad. There was an absurd protest by a professor, who I think was named González, because the Rómulo Gallegos Prize was given to the young, Europeanized Vargas Llosa rather than to the truly heroic Spanish American novelists such as this or that one, who had been awaiting their laurels for decades. Articles by Argentines in Colombian journals, by Colombians in Uruguayan journals, by Uruguayans in Cuban journals would bring their authors a certain renown by constituting the famous literary *trottoir*, denigrating those novelists who were most famous at the moment. These critics did the writers the signal favor of organizing them for the first time into that unity called the Boom; and, having been installed on a polemical plane, the Boom transcended the purely literary to become, more or less, gossip in the street. This adverse publicity and the explosion of *One Hundred Years of Solitude* in the second half of the '60s have resulted in making the Spanish American Boom something very ambiguous, which, when it did flow over, ran out of the classrooms, the anthologies, the erudite studies, the texts, the schools, the specialists.

And after 1965, with this new high point of the novel freed from its traditional heroic and civic duties and completely on its own, we enter fully into a more complex period—more contradictory but also more irreverent and open to contamination—in order to search for new levels of seriousness. It was the golden age of the Beatles, whose unity, then, seemed as definitive as that of this continental Boom of the novel, that at the beginning—according to the way I see it—had its seat in Mexico, in and around the disparaged Mafia of Carlos Fuentes' friends. We were reading Susan Sontag and *Lie Down in Darkness* and Baldwin; we were discovering Broch and Arrabal and Lukacs; we were talking about *camp*, *trivia*, *op*, *pop* and *gestalt;* the total boredom with the *nouveau roman* and the "happenings" began; and the indignation toward the use of napalm in Vietnam and toward the invasion of Santo Domingo; we saw United States draft cards being burned publicly; and we could not explain how a novel as extraordinary and complex as *Herzog* could remain for so long on the bestseller lists in the United States; and the Casa de las Américas [1] stretched out the flypaper of its generous invitations to intellectuals. I saw the first miniskirt of my life on the Paseo Juárez in Mexico City in 1965. I had been invited to participate in the Symposium of Intellectuals at Chichén Itzá in the Yucatán, a trip my wife and I began with the intention of staying abroad for only three months: after the Symposium we would jump to New York for the

[1] *La Casa de las Américas* was founded in 1960 in Havana after Fidel Castro came to power. It defines itself as "a cultural institution directed to serve all the peoples of the continent in their fight for freedom." *La Revista de la Casa de las Américas* is a literary and cultural magazine which brought together many Latin American writers. [G.K.]

launching of *Coronation* in English and then we would return to Chile. But we did not return.

It was Carlos Fuentes who, knowing that I was asphyxiated in my country, suggested my name to Bob Wool so that he would invite me to the Symposium at Chichén Itzá. In Chile my obsessive relationship with *The Obscene Bird of Night*, which I was unable to finish, was stifling me, but I did not want to burn it once and for all. In Chile I felt the sad and well-known discouragement of an underdeveloped country where it was necessary to find three or four different jobs in order to be able to write at least on Sundays and to keep myself afloat economically, knowing, consequently, that one is condemned to never writing anything of importance.

Leaving Chile and arriving in Mexico, reestablishing contact with Carlos Fuentes, meeting Juan Rulfo and Lillian Hellman and William Styron and Oscar Lewis and the whole flock of Mexican writers, I set myself entirely into motion again—as when I left my country to go to Princeton; as when I left for Buenos Aires—arousing my curiosity without frustrating it, feeding my hunger that had for so long gone unsatisfied. This enthusiasm at seeing myself surrounded by so many legendary people whom I knew through their work may have been infantile and naïve but no less valid to me for that. How could I forget Bette Davis in Lillian Hellman's *The Little Foxes?* How could I not want Styron to speak to me of his literary drought, which was lasting a decade after his first highly admired books? Quickly these characters were transformed into people: they ate in front of me at the table, they annoyed me when they came late to the work ses-

sions with tired faces, they asked my opinion on this or
that or simply asked me to light a cigarette.

The plane transporting the participants in the Symposium from Mexico City to Mérida began to nose dive
near the peak of Orizaba Mountain: furious, José Luis
Cuevas declared that he was not prepared to die in such a
stupid accident as this because the newspaper headlines
would only read "Tragic Air Accident in which Many
Famous Intellectuals Perish" with a list following where
his name would appear among many; and he cried, remembering all the flights on which he had missed the
chance to die, since the headlines would then have read
"Brilliant Painter José Luis Cuevas Perishes in Air Accident." One night Marta Traba enticed Juan Rulfo and
Robert Rossen into accompanying her in climbing one of
the Mayan pyramids: the North American, fairly drunk,
fell down the steps and was found in the underbrush by
Glauber Rocha, who dragged him to the hotel where
waiters decked out as Mayan gods were serving Yucatán
venison, fresh pineapple, and lobster mousse. Another
night—of this Symposium I remember the people, the
anecdotes, the splendor of the ruins and the jungle, but
absolutely nothing about the work sessions, which proves
definitively how useful international congresses are for novelists—tipsy with tequila and whisky and with superb
daiquiris, a group caused a tremendous uproar in a corridor of the hotel playing trivia games, which had just become popular: who played the role of Prissy in *Gone With
the Wind?* who did the lighting for *Philadelphia Story?* who
married the fashion designer Adrian? Being able to answer
some of these totally absurd questions confirmed, in a

93

way, my feeling of belonging to an international and contemporary generation—Uruguayans and North Americans, Peruvians and Mexicans—since we were all participating in the same cosmopolitan myths to whose characters we were alluding, and these trivial myths, so many of them revived by pop art, had a relevance to my generation at least as great as that of the heroic national myths. Cuevas and Styron were the unquestionable champions and were the ones who shouted the most when they played trivia in the hotel corridor. Suddenly, like the ghost of an explorer coming out of the jungle, with his white sideburns and a red face congested with anger, Alfred Knopf himself, my publisher in New York, appeared in his pajamas and condemned our frivolity making us be quiet with an angry diatribe that resounded in the tropical night emblazoned, just as in the movies, with fireflies. Serious intellectuals, during a Symposium, talking about Lupe Vélez playing the role of Cleopatra? In my provincial naïveté—and in spite of the Congress of Intellectuals in Concepción where the most memorable thing, outside of several meals with Neruda and Carpentier, was what was *not* done—I thought that writers at symposia should worry exclusively and directly about the vicissitudes and tragedies in the contemporary world, and that the most valuable part of a symposium is found only in the value of the papers presented. I realized that literary matters tend to wither away when they are directly formulated as problems to be solved and when only that dimension is granted them, because they are cut off from the metaphor, hidden or exposed, that necessarily is what is literary. I also realized how that metaphor can take, perfectly, the form of the tangential, the indirect, the allusive,

94

the trivial, the irrational hidden within pseudo-rational schemes like the one offered by this Symposium as a façade, a façade in which, in fact, nothing happened, but behind which a lot happened. I realized how, just as in the façades of Pinturrichio, the anecdotal or secondary detail is what remains in the end, much more deeply engraved or assuming greater importance than what is happening to the central character: how Marta Traba shook the bangs on her forehead and her up-to-date wardrobe; the solitary and affable Juan Rulfo, walking as if lost in the tropical night; the *camaraderie* more than the ideas expressed by Oscar Lewis, whose *Children of Sánchez* was at that time the most talked-about book in Mexico and perhaps in the world; Jay Laughlin going crazy laughing at some ironic comments by Nicanor Parra in a corner; the timidity of Dalmiro Sáenz, who, suddenly uprooted from his context and entirely stripped of his air of a Buenos Aires tough, seemed infinitely fragile to me; Lillian Hellman, during a presentation of *The Bald Soprano* in her honor, declaring that she never went to the theater because she did not like it.

These were the descriptive, perhaps superficial, things that occurred in the dazzling Mexican carnival that completed another stage of my liberation as a writer. The carnival culminated with the party the Mexicans gave for the foreigners at Carlos Fuentes' home in Mexico City. The confusion and clamor were presided over by Rita Macedo, the beautiful actress who was Carlos Fuentes' wife: an ecstatic, untouchable goddess, it was as if the cultural officials had lent her for the occasion like some very valuable piece from the recently opened National Museum of Anthropology in Mexico City. In a corner of the overcrowded room, Kitty de Hoyos, a starlet of Mexican films, took the stiff, Puritan hand of Rodman Rockefeller and passed it over her hips, while behind his glasses, the Yankee millionaire's eyes bulged with surprise and acute sensation. "Here, touch, so you don't have to keep looking," the actress was saying. To the unforgettable sound of "I Want to Hold Your Hand," which could hardly be heard above the uproar, Erika Carlson, Arabella Arbenz— the daughter of the ex-president of Guatemala—and China Mendoza were dancing wildly, the latter almost completely stripped of her garnet velvet dress, her gloves, and her black lace stockings. The *tarántulas* absorbed even the most timid people in the ribbon of bodies caught up in the breathless rhythm in which the beautiful ladies were losing one piece of clothing after another. Nicanor Parra and Juan Rulfo were ridiculing it all; Sonia Vidal sang something and I searched through the rooms and gardens for Gabriel García Márquez because in Chichén Itzá I had read *No One Writes to the Colonel* with astonishment and because someone had said "Gabo's at this party." At the moment when I was passing the information along to my wife so that she could help me find him, a man with a black mustache came up to me and asked if I were Pepe Donoso; as we embraced in the Latin American manner, the frenzied *tarántula* passing by absorbed us too.

We were unable to continue talking on that occasion, but we did afterwards. According to what he told me, García Márquez was experiencing a literary dry spell, one that had lasted for nearly ten years. He could not come out of it. His books circulated in very small circles. At least I had the prospect, with *Coronation* soon to be published in the United States, that I was going to be able to feel some stimulus to bring about the necessary synthesis in order to finish *The Obscene Bird of Night*. I saw García Márquez as a gloomy, melancholy person tormented by his writer's block, a blockage as legendary as those of Ernesto Sábato and the eternal block of Juan Rulfo which he has come out of with all the fame that is public knowledge—Rulfo affirms that he is not blocked; rather, that while he was a writer before, he is not one now.

I decided then not to return to Chile because if I did it was going to perpetuate my obsessive relation to my novel while I rotted away in the various jobs which got me nowhere. I stayed in Mexico with my wife, to write what I could, during the three months before we had to go to New York for the launching of *Coronation*. We moved into the guest house that Carlos Fuentes rented to us in the rear of his garden on Galeana Avenue.

In a few weeks I was already writing *Hell Has No Limits*. I would not, could not, continue to be obsessed by my long novel: in order to unblock myself it was necessary to write something else, perhaps something shorter. For this purpose, I tore out an episode of about a page in length from one of the many versions of *The Obscene Bird of Night*, which, when enlarged, was converted in the space of two months into *Hell Has No Limits*. Seated in the shade of the guest house at the back of the garden I typed it. At the other end of the garden, in the large house, with Vivaldi's *Seasons* playing as loud as the stereo could go, Carlos Fuentes was writing *A Change of Skin*. My wife, at her table in the garden, was typing, translating Jules Feiffer's *Harry Is a Rat with Women*. And underneath Fuentes' study, next to a window that overlooked the garden, as aloof and wise as an enchantress who was stitching the multicolored pieces of our literary destinies, Rita Macedo, with her sewing machine, was making sumptuous dresses for herself and for their daughter Julissa, who was then beginning her movie career.

To show on what economic level I and nearly all the writers of my generation in Chile and perhaps in the other small countries of Latin America were accustomed to working, I should say that I think one of the reasons why my large novel was blocked and remained that way for so many years was because Zigzag Publishers, owners of the magazine *Ercilla*, of which I was the editor for so many years, had loaned me in 1960 the exorbitant sum of one thousand dollars against the collateral of a possible, un-stipulated, and still unbegun novel that I was to write for them someday. That thousand dollars was spent for air-plane fare to Europe—for the Chilean-Italian Prize which did not include travel expenses—where, for almost a year, I sent back interviews and articles for *Ercilla*. But I was left with the debt, desperately attempting to pay it off. And since a thousand dollars seemed an exorbitant sum to us in Chile at that time, the only way to settle the debt and escape the generous clutches of Zigzag was by writing *The Obscene Bird of Night*. The force of that necessity, mag-nified a thousand times by the economic conditions in which I was living, left me paralyzed for a long time: I was incapable—any writer in my part of the world was in-capable—of producing a thousand dollars with my literary work. But in Mexico I began to think that in the end there was no reason that it had to be my "great" novel. Why not something shorter, less important to me, something that would cost less effort and would free me from my slavery? When all was said and done and seen from a *non*-Chilean perspective, a thousand dollars was not really that much.

After the anguish of Chile, those months in the guest house at the back of the garden on Galeana while I was writing *Hell Has No Limits* were extraordinary. The healthful way I had discovered to free myself from the slavery of Zigzag's thousand dollars, from the tremendous obsession of paying them with my most complex and involved novel, gave me a feeling of lightness, of lucidity, of digging myself out: that thousand dollars was nothing more than a symbol of dependence and isolation, of pride and the lack of stimulation and hope of the writers who were not becoming international in the full sense of the world. My commitment to Zigzag was, in the last analysis, unstipulated and partial. Besides, it was clear that whenever they wanted to, Zigzag obtained free tickets for their correspondents, and that during the year abroad I was sending back exclusive interviews with Ezra Pound, with Giorgio de Chirico, with Elsa Morante, with Bulatovic while I was also reconstructing the world of Joyce and Svevo in Trieste and the world of Lampedusa in Palermo. Looked at closely, all this was not bad work. Why did I think that I owed Zigzag my entire self and not just a part of myself, something like the short novel I wrote in the house on Galeana?

All the picaresque literary-plastic-cinematographic-theoretical-social elements in Mexico, not to mention the world, paraded through Carlos Fuentes' and Rita Macedo's house. Publishers from the United States, literary agents, directors of movies, magazines, and companies all passed through. Besides the invitations from Cuba came the dignitaries like Roberto Fernández Retamar, who dazzled the Mexican world with his cultural refinement. Jorge

99

Ibargüengoitia and Augusto Monterroso made irreverent jokes about the heavy epic burden of Latin American history and literature. All curves, wigs, and dyed fox, La Tongolele attended lectures by the new batch of Mexican writers at the Palace of Fine Arts. In the house on Galeana they begin to shoot a film in which Julissa and Enrique Alvarez Félix played the leading couple in *Las dos Elenas* (The Two Elenas) based on a short story by Carlos Fuentes: the house on Galeana was a confusion of make-up artists, hair stylists, lighting directors, extras, photographers, onlookers. And then began that extended and boring period during the filming when everything is tentative, when something is always missing—a certain kind of dress, a curtain, a double bed (which one fine morning they stole right out from under our warm bodies because it was the only double bed in the house)—and where someone unexpected always arrived, delaying everything: the great María Félix, for example, the first lady of Mexican cinema, who suddenly appeared to give a little friendly kiss to the cameraman, Gabriel Figueroa, and to see how her son, Enrique, was acting. He, swinging on Cecilia Fuentes' swing while my wife and I listened, told Carlos Fuentes many of the anecdotes with which Fuentes would later construct *Holy Place*. The ending of *Las dos Elenas* was filmed several months later in New York—where my wife and I arrived simultaneously with that cinematographic carnival to attend the launching of *Coronation* by Alfred Knopf—in a spectacular party at the St. Regis, where Fuentes assembled his personal New York *Who's Who* from Princess Lee Radziwill to Jules Feiffer—Salvador Dali had asked for ten thousand dollars to walk across the screen with his domesticated panther and so his services were dispensed with—and where we all appeared as extras.

When in 1965 I proposed my course on the contemporary Spanish American novel in translation to the University of Iowa's Writers Workshop, Vance Bourjaily told me that it might be preferable to do a course on poetry since that was our literary form with the greatest prestige abroad, while the novelists were unknown and of no interest to anyone. I heatedly defended my point of view and won. I do not think that I am very mistaken in asserting that one of the things that marks the "contemporary" era of Latin American literature is, precisely, this change: our poetry, garlanded with monumental names like Pablo Neruda, César Vallejo, Octavio Paz, Rubén Darío, and Nicanor Parra, ceases to be so active as a literary form perhaps because the public receptive to poetry is now too exclusive and too academic; and, at the same time, the novel, liberated from its civic and pedagogical bonds, is showing itself to be infinite and varied in its capacity to attract an international audience and has advanced suddenly to the first rank to occupy the favored position previously occupied by poetry.

What this does *not* mean is that our contemporary novel is superior to, say, the French, Spanish, or English novel: that is a competitive, infantile topic, lacking importance. I do firmly believe that for Latin Americans the novel has suddenly been transformed into *the* artistic form *par excellence*, the form which characterizes the artistic world during the 1960s; as lyric poetry written in Spain during and a little after the 1930s characterized that period; and as the murals painted in Mexico characterized the 1920s. In the 1960s, the novel came to fit the Latin American moment like a glove. I realize that poetry written in Spanish in the 1930s produced things which will probably be immortal—if that unpopular word still has relevance—something which in relation to the present-day Spanish American narrative is still not at all clear. On the other hand, I realize that the Mexican murals have become sadly impoverished with time and that today the overload of gesturing and pedagogical rhetoric has lost all its eloquence—something that very well may happen to the Boom in one or two decades. But for the moment, and this was what was so exciting, to have a Spanish American novel in hand was to feel, more than with any other form, the throbbing of something alive.

In any case, today, seven years later, Vance Bourjaily could not tell me what he told me at the University of Iowa: *Hopscotch, Three Trapped Tigers, Betrayed by Rita Hayworth, One Hundred Years of Solitude,* and *Bomarzo* have all distinguished themselves in the United States recently. Surely one of the most moving experiences that a work of art can provide is the embodying of what is contemporary, not the formulating of it. Since the Spanish American novel embodies the contemporary in so many ways, I confess that at times I fear its quickly passing out of style. My fear diminishes, however, when I reflect how perhaps that will not take place because the novel has not postulated theories or positions but, rather, has simply happened, has burst forth as a natural growth. Passing out of style, the Boom as a unity will not leave behind a skeleton of theories but, instead, maybe a half dozen novels that have not been eclipsed. In the long run it will probably turn out that neither the contemporary Spanish American novel nor the novelists who most figure in it are the best or the greatest of our time. But that does not matter: the adventure was worth the effort. I would only like to state that during the '6os the novel was the form of the artistic effort which characterized Latin America.

In the garden on Galeana Avenue in Mexico, after spending five years circling and circling around myself, attempting to catch *The Obscene Bird of Night*, I succeeded in finishing *Hell Has No Limits*. When he read the original, Carlos Fuentes suggested that it was too good to use to pay off an absurd debt of a thousand dollars in Chile, since it would never get out of that country because the publishing monopoly would prevent that. He recommended, rather, that I publish the book in Mexico where it would have greater exposure. The publishing house of Joaquín Mortiz, at that time new and active, became interested. Now that I had unblocked myself, it certainly would be very easy for me to write something to settle the famous debt while I was finishing *The Obscene Bird of Night* without disturbances. To publish in Spanish outside of Chile meant, at least symbolically, a liberation: to cease to be dependent upon the monopoly of Chilean enterprise and taste and to acquire a certain autonomy, that was what mattered.

In that period, the director of the magazine *Encounter* passed through Mexico and spoke of founding a great magazine for Latin American writers, similar to *Encounter* and based in Paris. On his journey through Latin America, which he was then just beginning, he unquestionably would encounter numerous people suitable to the task. Actually, in Montevideo he contacted Emir Rodríguez Monegal and months later the first number of *Mundo Nuevo* appeared, a magazine which would count among its collaborators the writers most in view at the moment—except for Cortázar and Vargas Llosa who abstained—and who doubtlessly gave a clear shape to the Boom since the writers excluded from those pages were above all the ones who began to speak of a Mafia, of a pool of uprooted writers who lived olympically in foreign countries and who used *Mundo Nuevo* to share their formulas for success. During the years it was directed with talent and discrimination by Emir Rodríguez Monegal, this magazine exercised a decisive role in defining a generation. Some people contend that it had nothing to do with *Mundo Nuevo*, that it had nothing to do with Rodríguez Monegal; that the phenomenon, the effervescence of the Latin American novel of the '60s existed already and that *Mundo Nuevo* did not create anything but only brought things together and then "only partially" since Cortázar and Vargas Llosa never collaborated in its pages, even though frequent articles and reviews about the works of these writers appeared in it. Be that as it may, *Mundo Nuevo* was the voice of the Latin American literature of its time, and that could not have occurred by chance alone; rather a personal, discriminating vision, a knowledge of the whole, had to exist. For better or for worse, and with all the risk that my statement implies, I am convinced that the history of the Boom, at the moment in which it was most united, is written in the pages of *Mundo Nuevo* up to the moment when Emir Rodríguez Monegal abandoned its directorship. Of all the literary magazines of my time, from *SUR* to *La Revista de la Casa de las Américas*, and allowing for the necessary limitations of each one, none has succeeded in transmitting the enthusiasm for the existence of something alive in the literature of our period and of our world with the precision and amplitude of *Mundo Nuevo* at the end of the '60s.

7

FOR ME, the story of the Boom begins at the home of
Carlos Fuentes in 1965 with that spectacular party presided over by the hieratical figure of Rita Macedo, covered
with glitter and furs: that was the moment of the first out-
pouring, when everything seemed to be solidifying, from
the policy of rapprochement of the Cuban intellectuals,
uniting all of our part of the world with their promise of
freedom, to the founding of *Mundo Nuevo* with its base
aggressively located in Paris.

And for me, the Boom as an entity came to an end—if it
ever was an entity outside one's imagination and if, in fact,
it has ended—on New Year's Eve of 1970 at the home of
Luis Goytisolo in Barcelona with a party presided over by

María Antonia who, while weighed down by outrageous, expensive jewelry and in multicolored knickers and black boots, danced, bringing to mind a Leon Bakst model for *Scheherezade* or *Petrouchka*. Wearing his brand-new beard in shades of red, Cortázar danced something very lively with Ugne. In front of the guests who encircled them, the Vargas Llosas danced a Peruvian waltz and, later, the García Márquezes entered the same circle, which awarded them a round of applause, to dance a tropical *merengue*. Meanwhile, our literary agent, Carmen Balcells, lay back on the plump cushions of a couch, licking her chops and stirring the ingredients of this delicious stew, feeding, with the help of Fernando Tola, Jorge Herralde, and Sergio Pitol, the fantastic, hungry fish that in their lighted aquariums decorated the walls of the room. Carmen Balcells seemed to have in her hands the strings that made us all dance like marionettes, and she studied us: perhaps with admiration, perhaps with hunger, perhaps with a mixture of the two, just as she studied the dancing fish in their aquariums.

More than anything else that evening, the founding of the magazine *Libre* was talked about. (The magazine had been devised at Cortázar's home in Vaucluse when a convoy of Spanish American writers from Paris met in Avignon with a convoy of Spanish American writers from Barcelona to attend the premiere of *El tuerto es rey* (The One-Eyed Man Is King) by Carlos Fuentes, with Samy Frey and María Casares.) How *Libre* would be constituted by enlarging the restricted editorial board with which it began was discussed and rotating directors as well as a long list of contributing members were decided on. One could not help thinking of another party, a Mexican party with tequila and lots of paper flowers, which prophesied the founding of another magazine based, like *Libre*, in Paris: on that New Year at the Goytisolo's home in Barcelona there was also an atmosphere of hope and unity, of happiness and certainty, despite certain barbs from those who quickly began to feel excluded and despite the imprecise statements by some indiscreet people. A little later, the magazine broke up: the incredible Padilla case exploded in Cuba, shattering the broad unity that had for so many years sheltered an entire spectrum of Latin American intellectuals, separating them now into politically, literarily, emotionally bitter and irreconcilable groups. With all its uproar, the Padilla case put an end to the unity that I saw flower for the first time among Latin American intellectuals when the Boom was just getting underway there at that Congress of Intellectuals in Concepción in 1962.

How long did the Boom last? Or does it still continue? Did it begin with the appearance of *The Lost Steps* and *Pedro Páramo*, let us say, in order to give it greater scope, and does it continue to the present? Or did it begin with *Mundo Nuevo* and end with the founding of *Libre?* Or might it have begun back in 1962 with the Congress of Intellectuals in Concepción and the angry protest against the mutual ignorance of the literature of Latin American nations? Maybe this protest worked so well that now every Latin American novel belongs and will belong to the Boom which will prolong itself, becoming bulkier and bulkier, until the end of time? I have no idea. I imagine that the professors and specialists will clarify these matters as perspective is acquired and as time, little by little, alters our view of the beginning and the end and as some novels, which seem prominent to us today, wither with time while others, which we were unable to see, come into view. Here in these notes I can only offer limited testimony, communicate my prejudices and enthusiasm, a very partial reality since it is focused from my very limited personal point of view. With time, the specialists will decide which names do and do not belong to a Boom of such debatable existence. Above all, during the last years, this Boom has been transformed into an ornamented circus wagon, with a somewhat undefined, rather battered shape and a bad reputation, which, nevertheless, everyone tries to mount, or at least onto which many publishers and critics try to push the new novelists, awarding prizes to any Spanish American novel and mystifying the public by annexing it—often without either the author's knowledge or desire—to the Boom, which is now so overpopulated that its boundaries are impossible to fix or to define.

Another curious fact should be added: that just at the end of the 1960s a schism occurred in the publishing house of Seix Barral that was indissolubly connected to the Boom. This schism produced Barral Publishers and Seix Barral and thus broke up the most influential agent for the internationalization of the Spanish American novel during the past decade. The date of this split more or less coincides with the famous New Year's Party at the house of Luisa María Antonia Goytisolo, with the founding of *Libre*, with the dispersion and disillusion resulting from the Padilla case. Some people speculate that this split within the most prestigious publishing house of my generation was not an accident but, on the contrary, that it was produced by Carlos Barral himself when he frivolously wanted to draw the definitive line so that the Boom would fit precisely into one epoch. Others contend that the schism was due to the discovery of a plot that it was necessary to terminate immediately: the Catalan members of the Biblioteca Breve Prize intended to destroy the Spanish novel by awarding one prize after another to Latin American novels written, at times, in rather curious variants of Spanish in order to eliminate definitively the tyranny of the Spanish language of Valladolid and of the novels written in that despised language. (It is curious to note that the jury who helped build the fame of the Latin American novel by giving it five out of ten Biblioteca Breve prizes was constituted basically of Catalans: Castellet, Clotas, Félix de Azúa, Carlos Barral are four judges whose first language is Catalan, as opposed to the rest of the jury composed of Juan García Hortelano, Gabriel García Márquez, and Mario Vargas Llosa whose first language is Spanish.) But the literary scene in Barcelona is full of rumors, secrets, theories, and everyone understands perfectly that when someone says, "Promise me, but really promise me that you won't tell anyone . . . what they go around saying is terrible," it is no more than a link in the chain of rumors weighing down the city and, consequently, that very little of what is postulated as ironclad truth can be believed.

Based on a small group of friends surrounding Carlos Fuentes in Mexico, Luis Guillermo Piazza published *La mafia* (The Mafia), a historical account with a very "in" tone, as he used to say in those years, grounded in the gossip surrounding that exclusive and envied group. It was this book that began the black legend of the sinister clique of writers devoted to mutual praise. Then, in a much more serious manner, *Into the Mainstream* by Luis Harss brought together several years ago ten writers who seemed at that time definitive in the literary panorama but whose primacy in regard to fame and literary quality in several cases seems debatable only a few years later.

But of all the suppositions surrounding the Boom, none is as burning, none as painful, none as ticklish as the question of the constitution of the Boom, of who does and does not belong, of who belongs in which category if it is even accepted that the Boom has categories. If categories are accepted, four names make up the kernel, the *gratin*, of the famous Boom in the eyes of the public, and they were and continue to be the most exaggeratedly praised and criticized as the supposed Mafia bosses: Julio Cortázar, Carlos Fuentes, Gabriel García Márquez and Mario Vargas Llosa. The public suspects that they are inseparable friends with identical literary tastes, with similar political positions, each one the master of a particular court which will follow him until death, all living in great comfort in foreign capitals and rubbing elbows with "the cream of the intellectuals"; but, of course, this is naïve and false, as false as the notion of stagnation in human and political relations, as false as the idea of perpetual unanimity of opinions expressed by individualists as spirited as these writers are accustomed to being. Besides, as Oriane de Guermantes knew very well, the *gratin* seen from outside, and the reasons for inclusion or exclusion, and the persons included or excluded, are more than anything mirages seen by those who are excluded and want to belong. With works of high quality, which, in addition to being widely circulated and translated into many languages, have also exerted a powerful influence on one another and on writers in other categories of the Boom, this quartet of names unquestionably forms the *gratin*, the very core of the Boom. But this core that includes only four names could not, certainly, fill an entire literary decade of a continent. Thus, in order for the Boom to acquire greater size and solidity, it has annexed several older writers who are literarily connected to those of the *gratin* and who are indisputably great writers, although because of their age and orientation, they would not fit within the Boom: Borges, for example, despite his not writing novels and his reactionary political positions which would be incompatible and unacceptable; Juan Rulfo and Alejo Carpentier who, ripe ever since the beginning of time, seem to have been waiting for someone to harvest them; the private and secretive figure of Onetti; and, finally, José Lezama Lima, a Cuban advanced in years, the last brilliant flash, coming in time to form part of this second category which could be called the "proto-Boom," a category that along with the core would form the most clearly defined and least disputed categories of the Boom.

Later, the categories begin to fade somewhat and become more confused. Should not Ernesto Sábato, for example, belong to the *gratin* in his own right, since his success in certain European countries has been indisputably greater than that of some of the writers of the *gratin*, even though he insists on excluding himself, to the point of blocking the publication of *Sobre héroes y tumbas* in English for over a decade? Does not Guillermo Cabrera Infante also belong to the *gratin?* He has masterfully translated his *Three Trapped Tigers* into English and French by himself and thus caused the entire world to talk, so does he not deserve, consequently, to be included in the core of the Boom? For some reason, whether because they voluntarily exclude themselves or because the public listens to the legends and sees them as marginal, the position of these novelists is fluctuating and disputed: in any case, it can be accepted that, at the edge of the core and of the "proto-Boom" and belonging or not to those categories for reasons which can be as literary as extraliterary, these names give great variety and splendor to the phenomenon of the Boom.

Continuing with this dangerous classification—that should not be taken too seriously but rather as a more or less entertaining game—I would say that the public next sees a large number of writers—all with solid reputations, with acclaimed translations, and whose names reach, in some areas more than in others, the entire Spanish-speaking world—grouped a little below the main body of the Boom and consisting of Augusto Roa Bastos, Manuel Puig—the most brilliant of the group—, Salvador Garmendia, David Viñas, Carlos Martínez Moreno—whose novel *Con las primeras luces* (With the First Lights) deserves greater recognition—, Mario Benedetti, Vicente Leñero, Rosario Castellanos, the Chileans Jorge Edwards and Enrique Lafourcade, Augusto Monterroso, Jorge Ibargüengoitia, Adriano González León, in addition to other names which escape me at the moment, as the society page writers say.

Further down would come the "junior Boom": that is, those who, as Françoise Wagener assured the readers of *Le Monde*, belong to a younger generation and are searching out new routes for the Latin American novel after the great names of the Boom, but whose work is still scant, or known only in certain parishes: the French newspaperwoman headed this category with the names of José Emilio Pacheco, Gustavo Sáinz, Nestor Sánchez, Bryce Echenique, and Sergio Pitol.

Parallel to the category I have called the "body of the Boom" and reaching at times above and below it but, in any case, apart from it, would come the enclosed "petit-Boom" of the contemporary Argentine novel, very important and very rich, but perhaps due to a certain arrogance that for so long produced an oligarchical literature, or perhaps due to the confusion introduced in the Perón years and lasting to the present, it has not succeeded in incorporating itself suitably into the rest of the Latin American novel, always remaining a little to the side, governing itself with its own proud laws: Manuel Mújica Laínez—whose *Bomarzo* was reviewed by Edmund Wilson himself in the pages of the *New York Review of Books*, an honor which very few can claim, Bioy Casares, Pepe Bianco, Murena, Beatriz Guido, Sara Gallardo, Elvira Orphée, Juan José Hernández, Dalmiro Sáenz, and so many others who form the very rich panorama of the Argentine novel of today but who, whether voluntarily or for other reasons, remain secret and whose names do not flow throughout the Spanish-speaking world as they should.

Finally comes the "sub-Boom": obviously homemade reputations, names launched by scarcely solvent prizes which display showy bands on books announcing the very rapid sale of ten editions, which no one disputes but which no one cares about either. It is in this category that rancor and envy develop; here, among those who want and cannot or do not quite know what they want; they are the ones who support the enmities and quarrels; they are the ones of identical nationality who do not realize the international breadth open to the Latin American novel today and who, because they are compatriots and are so weighed down with envy that they feel nothing for a novelist from another country, remain mentally provincial, even though they may live in France, let us say. Their perpetually competitive stance makes them each moment more impotently conscious of the thousands of steps they still have to take to reach some fellow countryman settled at the core of the Boom, which, of course, they reject as both a core and a literary quality.

I repeat that I am offering this classification of the Boom more than anything else as a kind of game, and that I do not pretend to have named everyone who should be included in each category. In any case, the status of the Boom is in a crisis as it has always been; but it is a crisis produced by overabundance, by noise and scandal, by the demographic explosion of the novelists who are or who were linked within the Boom, by the loss of order and direction, until finally by the time we enter the '70s everything has been transformed into an indiscriminate conglomeration where it is very difficult to perceive values and to judge. I repeat that certain young novelists say of so-and-so that "he writes almost as badly as Cortázar"; and if the latter's imitators proliferate, so do his detractors, entrenched behind the name of Lezama Lima: the fight between the Cortazarian novelists and the Lezamists promises to bear delicious fruit in this decade. Despite *A Change of Skin*'s receiving a Biblioteca Breve Prize, Carlos Fuentes, for obvious reasons, is relatively little known in Spain, and his presence within the core of the Boom may be more disputable than the presence of the other three. The silences following the great novels, which seem to have exhausted their authors' worlds (as in the case of *One Hundred Years of Solitude*) cause hopeful enemies to count the months that pass in which the author's next, promised novel is not published and to predict with pleasure the total and final drought, as in the case of Juan Rulfo, whom everyone now loves and admires because he no longer writes. The new generation finds the novel of the '60s excessively literary, and they devote themselves, like those in all avant-garde movements, to writing an "anti-literature," an "anti-novel." Among those under forty there are novelists full of energy who produce brilliant and appetizing novels: Manuel Puig and, despite his belonging to the core of the Boom, Mario Vargas Llosa, both interested in film, both with similar and novel visions.

Perhaps, yes; perhaps the Boom is in crisis, but, after all, it is enough: the things which maintained that precarious cohesiveness are lacking now, if they really did exist at one time. Perhaps the moment has passed and we no longer have to continue talking of the Boom; we can stop shoving one another in trying to climb on the ornamented wagon whose journey is still followed by some glittering stars. Puff! The Boom has been a game; perhaps more precisely, a cultural broth that nourished the tired form of the novel in Latin America for a decade. The Boom will disappear—already it is less spoken of—and three or four or five excellent novels will remain that will recall it and for which so much scandal and so much fuss have been worth the trouble. Which novels will remain? And how long will they last? That, luckily, is not known. Meanwhile, we go on struggling in order to write more and more things that may be born in an already endangered condition; or, on the contrary, that will give birth to new things when it was thought no longer possible—as in the case of Lezama Lima.

With these notes I do not pretend to have even scratched the surface of what the Boom has been and even less to have asserted a theory about it. Most likely, I have excluded entire movements, entire countries, very important names: nearly all are excluded through simple ignorance or forgetfulness. And so much more could be said, as much by way of anecdote as by theory. But perhaps the moment has not yet arrived and we do not know how to measure nor to choose. In any case, my experience of the Boom—whatever may be the category to which I belong—has been of a passionate, committed interest which could easily distort the perspective of what I have said here. And although many of these pages may seem to be a laughing matter, I feel so identified with the adventure of the internationalization of the novel of the 1960s that in giving my testimony about it I have found myself, at times, writing parts of my autobiography.

Calaceite, 1971

INDEX

119